The Quest for Better Rest

The Quest for Better Rest

Sleep Solutions from an ADHDer

by Aiden Ashlyn

Edited by Rebecca Henderson

Published by

Aiden Ashlyn

First Edition: December 2023
Book 1 of The Quest Series

Published by Aiden Ashlyn, LLC
Del Valle TX 78617
https://aidenashlyn.com/contact-us

Edited by Rebecca Henderson
Graphic design by Laurie Douglas
Cover illustration created using MidJourney AI

Printed in the United States of America
ISBN: 979-8-8719059-8-2

Gratitude

Special thanks to Kathleen Sperduti for
helping me realize my dream. Thanks and love to Laurie
Douglas for all her contributions. Thanks to my friends and
family who support me with their love, kindness, and compassion.
And most importantly, thank you to the readers of this book
for the opportunity to share it with you. May you find the
information helpful and my words supportive as
you venture on your quest for better rest.

Good Sleep = Good Life

Table of Contents

Disclaimer — 1

Introduction — 2

Chapter 1. Sleep and ADHD: The Basics — 4

The Importance of a Full Sleep Cycle — 6

Introduction to ADHD — 8

Three Types of ADHD — 9

How Prevalent is ADHD? — 9

Treating ADHD — 10

ADHD and Sleep: What's the Connection? — 12

Chapter 2. Sleep Problems and Their Impact on ADHD Symptoms — 14

Sleep Deprivation and ADHD Symptoms — 14

Common Sleep Problems — 15

Sleep Deprivation and ADHD — 18

Emotional Dysregulation and Behavior Problems — 19

The Impact of Sleep Deprivation on Executive Function, Attention, and Impulse Control in People with ADHD — 20

Chapter 3. The Impact of ADHD on Sleep — 22

The Bidirectional Relationship of Sleep Problems and ADHD — 23

Three Ways ADHD Affects Sleep — 23

Neurobiological Factors — 24

Dysregulation of Neurotransmitters — 25

Brain Structure and Function — 26

Behavioral Factors — 27

Medication Factors — 29

Stimulants — 30

Non-Stimulants — 31

Chapter 4. Sleep Hygiene for ADHDers **33**

Sleep Hygiene Begins As Soon As You Wake Up 33

The Circadian Clock *34*

Sleep Hygiene Habits for the Evening 37

Yoga Nidra 40

The Five Layers of Self *41*

Five Reasons to Incorporate Yoga Nidra into Your Nightly Routine *41*

Chapter 5. Treating Sleep Problems with Medication **44**

First Steps 45

Over-the-Counter Sleep Medications 46

Some Precautions *46*

1. Diphenhydramine *47*

2. Doxylamine *48*

3. Melatonin *48*

Potential Benefits *49*

Possible Side Effects *50*

Prescription Medications 50

Antidepressants *52*

Benzodiazepines (Benzos) *52*

Nonbenzodiazepines, Also Known as Z-Class 54

Choosing the Right Medication 55

How to Stop Taking Prescription Sleep Medications 55

Chapter 6. Cognitive-Behavioral Therapy for Sleep Problems **57**

What is Cognitive Behavioral Therapy for Insomnia (CBT-I)? 57

CBT-I Addresses the Following Areas that Typically Contribute to Persistent Insomnia. *58*

How It Works: CBT-I Interventions 60

Cognitive Restructuring *60*

Stimulus Control *61*

Sleep Restriction and Compression *62*

Progressive Muscle Relaxation *63*

Hypnosis 63

Self-Hypnosis 64

Biofeedback 65

Autogenic Training 65

Breathing Exercises 66

Relaxation Training 67

Sleep Hygiene and Related Behaviors 67

Homework 67

Chapter 7. Complementary and Alternative Medicine for Sleep Problems 69

Supplements 70

Five of the Most Common Supplements for Sleep 70

Melatonin 70

Magnesium 71

Valerian 71

Cannabidiol (CBD) 72

Glycine 73

Aromatherapy 74

How Does Aromatherapy Work? 74

How to Use Essential Oils 74

Which Essential Oils Are Used to Treat Insomnia? 75

Acupuncture 76

How is Acupuncture Performed? 77

Acupuncture for Sleep 77

Acupressure 78

Emotional Freedom Technique (EFT) 79

Mindfulness Meditation 80

Chapter 8. Sleep Tips for Parents of Children with ADHD 83

Get Your Child Tested 84

Start with a Sleep Diary 84

Sleepiness Scale 85

Sleep Study   85

Blood Test   86

Sleep Hygiene   87

Bedtime Routine   87

Sleep Environment   89

Lifestyle Considerations   90

Food   90

Exercise   91

Falling and Staying Asleep   92

Chapter 9. New Parents, Teens, and Young Adults   **94**

New Parents   94

The Teen Years   95

Helping Your Teen Get More Sleep   97

College, Roommates, and Other Cohabitation Situations   99

Some Tips For Better Sleep   99

Chapter 10. Advice for Irregular Circumstances   **101**

Shift Work, Sleep Disorders, and ADHD   101

Air Travel   103

Before Travel   103

During Travel   103

After Travel   104

Supporting Your Partner   104

Autism   106

Conclusion   **109**

Resources   **113**

References   **117**

Disclaimer

The content of this book is for informational purposes only. It is not intended to diagnose, treat, cure, or prevent any condition or disease. Readers understand that this book is not a substitute for consultation with a licensed practitioner. Please consult your physician or healthcare specialist regarding the suggestions and recommendations made in this book. The use of this book implies your acceptance of this disclaimer.

The publisher and the author make no guarantees concerning the level of success you may experience by following the advice and strategies contained in this book, and you accept the risk that results will differ for each individual. The testimonials and examples provided in this book show exceptional results, which may not apply to the average reader. They are not intended to represent or guarantee that you will achieve the same or similar results.

Introduction

If you dream of falling asleep and staying asleep until your alarm goes off in the morning but struggle to make this a reality, this book is for you. Life can be wonderful for people like me with Attention-Deficit/Hyperactivity Disorder (ADHD). I embrace it as my superpower. However, ADHD can also make some things more challenging, and sleep falls under that category for millions of people. What makes it even more difficult is that it isn't just a one-way street—ADHD affects our ability to sleep, while lack of sleep worsens some of the less desirable traits of ADHD, thus leaving us stuck struggling to break the cycle.

I often wondered what it must be like to feel tired before 2:00 am, turn off my screens, and fall asleep. No procrastinating before bed, no hyper fixation on my game, no exploring rabbit holes on my phone, nothing keeping me awake—just relaxing into a peaceful slumber. Each night, I promised myself I would go to bed before midnight, and every morning, I regretted not following through. It's a cycle I tried to break for years before finally figuring out a combination of sleep solutions that worked for me.

Why does sleep matter?

I will answer that question more in-depth in the following chapters. Still, these are just a few of the known effects of insufficient sleep:

- ☐ It has been linked to the development and management of several chronic diseases and conditions, including type 2 diabetes, cardiovascular disease, obesity, and depression.

- ☐ It can affect how we learn and process information.

- ☐ It can compromise the immune system, making us more susceptible to illnesses from common colds to cancer.

- ☐ It can increase vulnerability to mental health issues.

- ☐ It can profoundly disrupt blood sugar levels.

- ☐ It can increase risks of accidents. The National Department of Transportation estimates that each year, drowsy driving is responsible for 1,550 fatalities and 40,000 nonfatal injuries in the United States (Harvard Health Publishing, 2017).

- ☐ Ultimately, it can decrease lifespan.

Getting quality sleep in sufficient quantities may be *the* best thing we can do for our overall health.

I'll be honest. If you have struggled with your sleep for years, no quick fix will magically grant you 8 uninterrupted hours. However, lifestyle changes, medication, and therapies can help you overcome years of dysfunctional sleep and put you on the path to restful nights once you find the right combination of strategies. I'm not a doctor or a pharmaceutical rep; I'm just an ADHDer with sleep problems who took my health into my own hands and did the research to fix my own difficulties. Now, I want to share my discoveries with you.

CHAPTER 1

Sleep and ADHD: The Basics

*"People with ADHD often have a special feel for life,
a way of seeing right into the heart of matters, while
others have to reason their way methodically."*

—Dr. Edward M. Hallowell (Dahl, 2023)

I struggle with going to sleep more often than I like to admit. Once I finally lay down and close my eyes, I can sleep just fine, but I often simply don't do that. Why not? Because there are so many more exciting things to do instead.

I've played *Call of Duty Mobile* in bed ALL night long during my work week more than a dozen times over the past two years. After 1 or 2 all-nighters, I removed it from my phone for weeks or months at a time. I tried to resist my impulses but always reloaded it for some "special occasion" or as a weekend reward.

And guess what happened?

I found myself in the same position of watching the dawn break through my window—completely surprised I'd been playing the game for 7 or 8 hours straight. That realization was not a great feeling when faced with an 8 to 10-hour workday ahead. And it's not just *Call of Duty*. Even the simplest, most mundane game could keep me up for hours. Removing all games from my phone has helped me go to bed earlier, but it still hasn't solved the problem. There's always something else to capture my attention.

I decided to write a book on sleep and ADHD because all the other books I've read left me with the feeling that my ADHD is what is wrong with me, when really, so much about it is what makes me (and you?) the awesome person I am. Still, some aspects of ADHD make things more challenging for me, and sleep is one of them.

If you or someone you care about is struggling with sleep issues and ADHD is at least partly to blame, this book is for you. It will help you better understand what is happening in the brain and body that makes sleep that much more complicated for people with ADHD, and then provide some tips and tools to hopefully make it a bit easier to get a good night's sleep.

Everyone sleeps, but how often do you really think about what's happening in your body while you're asleep? I don't spend much time thinking about something when it's going right. However, sleep is something that can often go wrong. So, let's talk about what sleep is, why it's essential, and how lack of sleep specifically affects those with ADHD.

So, what exactly is sleep?

Sleep is a natural process allowing the body to rest and recuperate; cells can replenish their energy supply, and the brain flushes toxins that have built up during the day. During sleep, inactivity gives the body time to repair and recover from injury and illness. It provides time for the brain to perform self-maintenance by reorganizing and categorizing memories and learned information (Cleveland Clinic, 2023c).

Experts still don't know the biological purpose of sleep. But they do know everyone needs it. It is as essential as food and water to our survival. Sleep affects nearly every tissue and system in the body, including the brain, heart, lungs, metabolism, immune function, and mood. Our health and well-being are greatly affected by our sleep.

Did you know that the brain stays active while you sleep?

Sleep helps form the pathways in your brain that help us learn and create new memories (NIH, 2023). To be at our best, we need to get decent amounts of quality sleep regularly.

The Importance of a Full Sleep Cycle

First, some technical information to help us better understand why a proper night's sleep is not the same as catching 20 minutes here and there throughout the day and night.

Sleep is divided into 2 main types: rapid-eye movement (REM) and non-rapid-eye movement (NREM).

NREM sleep is divided into three stages: N1, N2, and N3.

- [ ] **N1:** This is the lightest stage of sleep. It occurs right after falling asleep and typically only lasts a few minutes, accounting for about 5% of total sleep. Sometimes, during this phase, you may twitch, jerk, or "jump" in your sleep.

- [ ] **N2:** This is the second stage and is the longest, almost 45% of the total sleep cycle. Sleep is still light, and brain waves slow down, pausing between bursts of electrical energy. Experts think this might be your brain organizing memories and information. Your body uses this stage to prepare for deep sleep.

- [ ] **N3:** This is the deepest stage of NREM sleep, also known as Delta sleep. For adults, it should account for around 25% of the entire sleep cycle. Delta brain waves are slow but strong, and still produce electricity. N3 is when the body repairs injuries and reinforces the immune system. Getting enough sleep in this phase is crucial for waking up feeling rested. It was probably during this stage if you have ever awakened from a deep sleep confused about what's happening.

- ☐ **REM:** REM sleep is the stage where dreams happen and is named for the rapid movement of your eyes during this period. This stage makes up the remaining 25% of the total sleep cycle, but it doesn't happen all at once. The first REM cycle typically lasts around 10 minutes, and then each cycle gets progressively longer. If you wake up during this phase, you may feel temporarily paralyzed. Brain activity during this stage is similar to when awake (Cleveland Clinic, 2023c).

It is essential to sleep long enough to complete an entire sleep cycle to get the full benefits. Most people spend 1/3 of their day sleeping. The expert consensus is that most healthy adults need a minimum of 7 hours of sleep per night to function at their best, though actual needs can vary. Some people need more than 7 hours, but very few need less until their senior years (Suni & Singh, 2023).

For those of us who have trouble sleeping or who suffer from a chronic lack of sleep or poor quality sleep, the effects can be severe, including an increased risk of disorders such as high blood pressure, cardiovascular disease, diabetes, depression, and obesity, as well as a decline in the ability to concentrate (NIH, 2023). ADHD is a comorbid factor for insomnia, so sleep disturbances are no strangers to the ADHD community (American Academy of Sleep Education, 2020).

We will discuss the negative impact of sleep disturbances on people with ADHD in Chapter 2.

Introduction to ADHD

"I knew I had strengths that other people didn't have, and my parents reminded me of them when my teachers didn't see them."

—David Neeleman, Founder of JetBlue
and entrepreneur with ADHD (Tina, 2018).

I am an ADHD advocate and I firmly believe that it plays a huge positive role in making me the person I am today. I see some traits that others call symptoms as advantages.

I love thinking outside the box and discovering new and creative ways to solve problems. My ability to hyperfocus on something for hours on end serves me well at work and when trying to level up in my games. I am a risk-taker, spontaneous, and have a great sense of humor. I have learned over the years not to take myself too seriously.

That said, ADHD can sometimes make life difficult, and many people struggle with certain aspects of it more than others. Let's break down exactly what it is from a clinical perspective so that we can better understand how both ADHD and the treatments to manage its more difficult attributes are related to sleep difficulties.

ADHD is an acronym for Attention Deficit/Hyperactivity Disorder. It is classified as a neurodevelopmental diagnosis affecting children and adults but is most often diagnosed in childhood. It is characterized by inattention, hyperactivity, and impulsivity that can interfere with daily life. There used to be separate diagnoses for ADD and ADHD, depending on whether hyperactivity was present, but now, three different types have been identified, all under the ADHD umbrella.

THREE TYPES OF ADHD

1. **Predominantly inattentive presentation:** This presents difficulty
    staying on task, being organized, and focused. Some examples
    might be making careless mistakes or missing crucial parts of
    instructions, frequent difficulty staying focused on tasks or
    activities, not following through on tasks, schoolwork, or chores,
    difficulty keeping personal belongings organized, losing things,
    and forgetfulness.

2. **Predominantly hyperactive/impulsive presentation:** This
    presentation refers to having excessive energy, difficulty sitting
    still, being overly talkative, making decisions, or acting without
    first thinking through the consequences. Some attributes include
    fidgeting or tapping, difficulty waiting when taking turns,
    frequently interrupting others, and difficulty staying seated or
    completing activities quietly.

3. **Combined presentation:** Combined type ADHD has features of
    both inattentive and hyperactive/impulsive presentations
    (American Psychiatric Association, 2022).

HOW PREVALENT IS ADHD?

When ADHD was first diagnosed more frequently in the 1990s, there
was a lot of discussion about its legitimacy.

Was it just a case of kids being kids?

Over the last few decades, research has shown that it was not. ADHD
is now recognized worldwide as one of the most common
neurodevelopmental conditions in children. Worldwide, approximately
129 million children and adolescents between the ages of 3 and 17
years currently have a diagnosis of ADHD. Among adults, that number

rises to 366 million. In the United States, 8.7% of American children currently have an ADHD diagnosis (Wirth, 2023).

Treating ADHD

I will go into more detail about treatment options in later chapters, but I have included a section here for two main reasons. The first is that sometimes ADHD can negatively impact sleep quality, and treating those symptoms can help. The second reason is the opposite. Sometimes, the treatments that help with unwanted symptoms can harm sleep.

Many people, myself included, feel that ADHD is their superpower, and I am all about positive acceptance of neurodiversity. However, many people also experience aspects of their ADHD that make some things in life more difficult. They would like to alleviate these. That's where interventions come into play. As I mentioned earlier, I prefer to focus on the positive aspects of ADHD because I believe that how we think about things can impact how we feel about them. However, I also believe that knowledge is power, and the more you know about how your ADHD works, the more you can use it to your advantage.

1. **Behavior Therapy:** Behavior therapy/training is available for both caregivers and patients. When very young children are diagnosed, caregivers are often given training in behavior management techniques. It is typically encouraged to try behavior modification before venturing into medication, particularly with children under the age of 6.

   In young children, behavior modification can be as effective as medication. The benefits of parent/caregiver training are that they learn to understand their child's behavior better and find ways to encourage more positive behaviors that help improve the child's overall experience inside and outside the home.

Classroom intervention, school support, and peer support are encouraged for school-age children. Children and adolescents can receive support to help them manage their schoolwork, implement strategies for classroom and social situations, and improve things like organization and executive functioning skills.

Behavior modification treatment can also include help with sleep hygiene, leading to fewer sleep problems over time (CDC, n.d.).

2. **Medication:** Several medications have been approved for treating ADHD. They typically fall into two classes: stimulants and non-stimulants.

    a. *Stimulants:* This is the most common type of medication prescribed, with 70-80% of children taking them reporting fewer symptoms. However, these medications can sometimes have side effects, including decreased appetite and, yes, sleep disturbances (Cleveland Clinic, 2023c). Some brand names include Adderall, Ritalin, Vyvanse, and Concerta.

    b. *Non-Stimulants:* Non-stimulant ADHD medication has been approved since 2003. While not as fast-acting as stimulant medication, they can last longer, helping to manage symptoms for up to 24 hours (Miller, 2023). Some brand names include Strattera and Viloxazine.

    Finding the suitable formulation and dose for optimal results for both stimulant and non-stimulant options often takes trial and error.

3. **Combination:** These treatment options do not have to be either/or. A combination of behavior modification treatment and medication can produce optimal results for some people because they tackle different areas of need.

In the United States, 77% of children and adolescents diagnosed with ADHD receive treatment. 30% take medication only, 15% receive behavior modification treatment only, and 32% receive a combination (Wirth, 2023).

ADHD and Sleep: What's the Connection?

If I'm being honest, sleep is probably my biggest complaint about having ADHD, and I'm not alone. ADHD is associated with sleep difficulties in between 25% and 50% of people with ADHD. Sleep difficulties tend to start in childhood, with many kids suffering from nightmares. These problems increase around puberty, including less sleep and difficulty falling asleep (Pacheco & Dimitriu, 2023).

Consistent sleep abnormalities have not been found in people with ADHD. Some ADHD symptoms can mimic the effects of sleep disorders, which can cause sleep disorders to go undetected for long periods. Forgetfulness, difficulty concentrating, hyperactivity, and impulsive behaviors can all result from ADHD, sleep deprivation, or both.

Some researchers believe that ADHD-related sleep problems result from impaired alertness and regulation circuits in the brain. Still, others point to a delayed circadian rhythm with a later onset of melatonin production. Delayed sleep phase disorder, a circadian rhythm sleep-wake disorder, is prevalent in 73-78% of children and adults with ADHD (Bijlenga et al., 2019). Regardless of the cause, sleep problems make life difficult for children and adults with ADHD.

In Chapter 2, we will talk more about the effects of sleep deprivation on executive function, attention, and impulse control in people with ADHD and how sleep deprivation can lead to emotional dysregulation and behavioral problems.

CHAPTER 2

Sleep Problems and Their Impact on ADHD Symptoms

You turn off the lights and snuggle under the covers, ready to sleep, only to be kept awake by annoying chatter coming from your brain. Sound familiar?

Unfortunately, not only does it suck being unable to sleep well at night and waking up tired in the morning, but the lack of sleep can also worsen those parts of ADHD that can make life more challenging. If you suffer from chronic sleep deprivation, it's possible you don't remember how differently you feel after a good night's sleep. I hope this will no longer be the case after you've read this book and applied the suggestions.

Sleep Deprivation and ADHD Symptoms

Sleep deprivation has been found to make ADHD symptoms worse in both children and adults.

Why is that?

In Chapter 1, we looked at all the different things that happen in the brain and body during a complete sleep cycle. The brain sorts and stores new memories and information, clears out toxins, and heals itself and the body while you rest. If that process is cut short by not making it through an entire sleep cycle or because of multiple interruptions throughout the night, you wake up in the morning without the full benefits of a good night's sleep.

Think of it like clearing out a sink of dirty dishes. If you can wash, dry, put away the dishes, rinse the sink, and wipe down the counter before bed, you wake up to a clean, uncluttered kitchen in the morning. That's not always an easy task for ADHDers. But if you *can* clean up, it will take another full day of adding dirty dishes to the sink to make it cluttered again.

But if you start doing the dishes and get interrupted multiple times, you might wash half, leave them to drip-dry, and skip finishing the job. When you wake up the next day, the kitchen is still a mess and will just get worse as you pile today's dishes on top of yesterday's mess. This happens to your brain when it doesn't have enough time to finish its tasks overnight to set you up for a fresh start in the morning.

COMMON SLEEP PROBLEMS

Before we get into details about how your ADHD can be affected by sleep problems, we need to understand some of the most common sleep disturbances. If you're like me, you will recognize yourself in more than one.

1. **Insomnia:** Insomnia impacts millions of people worldwide. It is when you have ongoing difficulties falling or staying asleep or are experiencing early morning awakenings. Insomnia is temporary for some people, coming and going at random. Maybe you're worried about something or experiencing a stressful time, and having trouble sleeping is a symptom. We've all been there.

While annoying, temporary insomnia isn't as big a problem as chronic insomnia. Chronic insomnia is when these difficulties persist for long periods, sometimes even after whatever caused it is no longer an issue. In other words, the stress of exam week can potentially lead to months of sleeplessness.

Treatment: There are several treatment options for insomnia, starting with maintaining a consistent sleep schedule and practicing good sleep hygiene, which we will cover in detail in a later chapter. Treatments such as cognitive-behavioral therapy for insomnia (CBT-I) and certain sleep medications can also be effective (Deshong, 2022).

2. **Sleep Apnea:** Sleep apnea is a severe condition characterized by repeated disruptions in breathing during sleep. Two things can cause it: 1) something physically blocking the airway during sleep, or 2) when the brain's signals to breathe don't work as they should. Sleep apnea doesn't just make you tired the next day. It is significantly associated with heart disease, hypertension, and stroke (Mayo Clinic Staff, 2016).

    Treatment: Lifestyle interventions such as weight loss can treat some sleep apnea problems. Continuous positive airflow Pressure - CPAP machines with masks and surgery are other, more invasive treatment options.

3. **Restless Leg Syndrome (RLS):** It sounds fake, but it's not. Restless Leg Syndrome is a neurological condition characterized by uncomfortable sensations in the legs. These feelings usually occur in the evening or at night, triggering an irresistible urge to move them and making it tough to relax. It can make it hard to fall asleep or wake you while sleeping.

Treatment: Some medications help manage symptoms, as well as lifestyle modifications and relaxation techniques to alleviate symptoms (ADDA, 2022).

4. **Narcolepsy:** Narcolepsy is also a chronic neurological condition that disrupts the regulation of sleep-wake cycles. You may get sudden episodes of daytime sleepiness, sometimes accompanied by muscle weakness. It can also result in sleep paralysis and vivid hallucinations (Johns Hopkins Medicine, n.d.a). Not fun!

   Treatment: Most treatment strategies include medications.

5. **Parasomnias:** I'm not going to lie; this one sounds like the title of a horror movie. Parasomnias is a group of sleep disorders characterized by abnormal behaviors or experiences during sleep. Sleepwalking (somnambulism), night terrors, and REM sleep behavior disorder (RBD), where you physically act out your dreams, are examples.

   Treatment: Options depend on the specific disorder, but behavioral interventions, medication, or a combination of both are common (Cleveland Clinic, 2021c).

6. **Delayed Sleep Phase Syndrome (DSPS):** This one might be the most common for people with ADHD. It is so common that some researchers wonder if it is a cause of ADHD diagnoses in individuals over the age of 12. DSPS is when people go to sleep two or more hours past what a conventional bedtime would be— say going to bed at 1:00 am instead of 11:00 pm because their body is not sending adequate sleep signals—and then have difficulty waking up in the morning due to a lack of alert signals (Stanford Medicine, n.d.). I think this happened most nights when I was up late playing video games. I knew I should sleep, but I just was not tired.

Treatment: The most common treatment is bright light therapy to reset the circadian clock. Studies have shown wearing blue and green wavelength-blocking glasses in the evening may also help as the melatonin hormone is disrupted by blue and green light (Tossini, 2022).

Sleep Deprivation and ADHD

James, a 25-year-old teacher, has started seeing himself through his 5th-grade students. A late-diagnosed ADHDer, he has only begun to understand how he has been affected by it for years. He always thought that he was one of those people who is just a little distracted, a little too energetic, and who loves seeking out the new and exciting.

James had never been a great sleeper, even as a child, and his parents love to tell stories of how he woke up at 5:00 am for years as a toddler. They would set up a playpen at the foot of their bed so he could play safely while his parents slept a few extra hours. That habit of waking up early followed him throughout his adolescence and into adulthood. As he got older, he realized he wasn't only waking up early; he was also waking up multiple times throughout the night and rarely getting a full night's sleep.

After becoming a teacher, James began recognizing some of his traits as he worked with the ADHD students in his classroom. On days following a particularly rough night of sleep deprivation, he struggled to remember all the details of his lesson plans, was less patient with his students, and often had difficulty keeping track of his belongings. He grew restless, struggled to pay attention to his students, and could barely sit still. The clock seemed to stand still the entire school day.

James had managed to make up for his bouts of inattentiveness, hyperactivity, and lapses in memory as a student, but he struggled as a teacher. Children demand 100% all the time. James realized he needed to get his sleep difficulties and his unwanted symptoms of ADHD under control.

The consequences of sleep deprivation look very much like some of the traits of ADHD. Not getting enough quality sleep can lead to increased hyperactivity, impulsivity, and inattention.

Sound familiar?

These symptoms can be even more severe in people with ADHD. Lack of sleep can make it more challenging for individuals to focus, complete tasks, and regulate emotions. Finally, sleep deprivation can contribute to difficulties with memory and learning, which are already common challenges for individuals with ADHD.

EMOTIONAL DYSREGULATION AND BEHAVIOR PROBLEMS

Most people are cranky after a poor night's sleep, and people with ADHD are no different.

Bad moods and behavior changes are probably the two most obvious symptoms of sleep dysregulation, mainly because they don't just affect the person who can't sleep. People notice when their typically friendly colleague snaps over something small at work or a kid has a meltdown at school. Adults often manage their urge to act out better than children or teens. However, mood swings may still affect them and potentially their relationships with others.

Sleep deprivation can have a profound impact on "emotional dysregulation and behavior" in individuals with ADHD. Emotional dysregulation is a fancy way of saying someone is having difficulty controlling their emotions. They may overreact or react in ways that don't fit the situation, such as yelling over a minor incident or crying when someone says something mildly upsetting (Pacheco & Dimitriu, 2023). It can also show up as being easily frustrated, overwhelmed, and having difficulty calming down after an outburst.

Emotional dysregulation is a classic trait of ADHD. Add sleep deprivation to the mix, and someone who already has difficulty controlling their emotional responses may no longer be able to hold it together. Worse, these symptoms can sometimes be mistaken for other diagnoses, making it hard to know the underlying issue.

Sadly, sleep deprivation does not strengthen positive emotions, just negative ones. Not only does a lack of sleep make it more likely you will overreact to something, but it also makes it more likely you'll see everything in a more negative light, thinking things are worse than they are. One study showed that people who were sleep-deprived tended to avoid social contact. By the same token, the negative energy of sleep-deprived participants made others unconsciously avoid them (Cohut, 2019). Basically, you feel terrible, think everything is awful, and try to avoid being around other people. What a drag.

THE IMPACT OF SLEEP DEPRIVATION ON EXECUTIVE FUNCTION, ATTENTION, AND IMPULSE CONTROL IN PEOPLE WITH ADHD

First, a few definitions. Executive function refers to processes in your brain that help you plan, organize, and regulate your behavior. Attention refers to the ability to focus on something without being easily distracted by things other people easily ignore or zoning out after a short time. Impulsivity is acting without considering the consequences first.

Sleep deprivation can impair executive function, time management, and prioritizing tasks, making them more difficult. In kids, this can mean difficulty with things like figuring out how long it will take to complete a school project and what steps to take to get started. In adults, this can adversely affect work projects or the achievement of personal goals.

Sleep problems can cause decreased attention span and concentration. If you find it hard to focus at work for long periods on the best of days, being sleep-deprived will make things much worse. Finally, lack of sleep also makes it harder to control impulsive or risky behaviors. In adults, impulsive behavior can be as straightforward as impulse shopping, or lead to more complicated, even dangerous behaviors.

Adults with ADHD are more likely to engage in risky behavior, such as speeding, and have a higher rate of car crashes than the general population. In addition, there is a correlation between ADHD and addiction, such as substance abuse and gambling (Dimitriu, 2021). Impulsivity and adrenaline-seeking behaviors are worse when ADHD is untreated or when decision-making abilities are impaired, such as when one is sleep-deprived.

Now that we have a better understanding of how sleep disturbances can make our lives difficult and negatively impact some ADHD traits, it's time to turn the tables. In Chapter 3, we'll learn how ADHD might contribute to sleep troubles.

CHAPTER 3

The Impact of ADHD on Sleep

"Remember that you are not alone. There are others going through the same thing."

—Adam Levine, Singer of Maroon 5 (ADDitude, 2020)

Lily, a college freshman, struggles in almost all her classes. An energetic and engaged student during the day, she participates enthusiastically in classes and joins two university clubs in her spare time. She credits her ADHD for her curiosity and love of learning, leading her to approach all her classes with an open mind and a willingness to learn.

So why does she struggle to remember course material? She completes all the readings, takes notes, and attends all classes, yet often forgets key points. Is it her lack of sleep?

Lily struggles to quiet her racing mind at night despite feeling exhausted at the end of the day. She bounces from thought to thought, unable to calm her mind. The hyperactivity that she manages with ADHD medication during the day returns with a vengeance at night. Most nights, she experiences restless leg syndrome as well, causing her legs to move almost uncontrollably, keeping her from sleep.

As a few sleepless nights turned into chronic insomnia, Lily's ability to consolidate new memories from her classes eroded. Lily's lack of rest began to take a toll on her overall well-being. She found it increasingly difficult to concentrate during the day—her energy levels plummeted, and her mood became increasingly erratic. Simple tasks became monumental challenges, and her relationships suffered as her patience wore thin. The negative impact of her ADHD on her sleep was a vicious cycle, worsening both her daytime focus and nighttime rest. She understood that her sleep problems were affecting her ADHD but didn't realize that her ADHD was also negatively impacting her sleep.

The Bidirectional Relationship of Sleep Problems and ADHD

Sleep problems and ADHD have a *bidirectional* relationship. Basically, sleep problems can make the unpleasant parts of ADHD worse, and ADHD can make sleep problems more severe.

It's a bit of a Catch-22.

When you think about it, it makes sense. Both ADHD and sleep are processes that affect the brain, so, of course, they affect each other. In Chapter 2, we learned about the impact of sleep deprivation on the ADHD brain, so now it's time to understand how our ADHD brains can contribute to some of those sleep issues.

THREE WAYS ADHD AFFECTS SLEEP

1. **On a neurobiological level,** the actual way the brain works can affect sleep patterns, making it more difficult to fall asleep, stay asleep, and get the best sleep possible.

2. **On a behavioral level,** how ADHD manifests behaviorally can lead to patterns of behavior that aren't the greatest for sleep (Ahem, playing Call of Duty until dawn).

3. **ADHD treatments.** Some medications that help control unwanted symptoms of ADHD can make it difficult to sleep under certain circumstances.

I know it sounds like the odds are stacked against you ever getting a solid eight hours of sleep. But don't throw in the towel. Understanding the problem is the first step to managing it. Many people like me with ADHD have cracked the sleep code, and so can you.

Neurobiological Factors

To highlight the bidirectional nature of sleep disorders and ADHD, consider that many of the sleep disorders discussed in Chapter 2 are more common in people with ADHD. This has led researchers to wonder if the brain differences in those with ADHD are causing, or at least contributing to, the development of certain sleep disorders (Joiner, 2018).

ADHD is now considered a 24-hour condition. This term captures the reality for many people. It doesn't just impact how we interact with the world while we are awake, but it can also have an influence while we sleep.

Studies have shown that individuals with ADHD are more likely to suffer sleep disturbance than their non-ADHD peers. Children tend to have shortened sleep cycles, which become increasingly common during the teen years. Teenagers with ADHD are more likely to get insufficient sleep both on school nights and on the weekends, and they have more daytime sleepiness than their peers as a result (Becker, 2020).

What makes teen sleep disturbances so interesting is that, generally, teens begin to suffer from more sleep problems and daytime drowsiness —even those not diagnosed with ADHD. Yet, teenage ADHDers are *still* more likely to experience it than their neurotypical peers. Sleep issues continue in adulthood, with poorer sleep quality and higher rates of insomnia among adult ADHDers. One study from Norway showed that 66.8% of adults with ADHD had insomnia compared with only 28.8% of adults without (Becker, 2020). This has huge implications for the health and development of kids and teens. The research shows that many with ADHD start suffering from sleep disturbances as children and continue to be sleep-deprived for the rest of their lives. Knowing what we do about how important sleep is to the brain and also to the general development and growth of children and teens, ADHDers are at a disadvantage even while just lying in bed.

DYSREGULATION OF NEUROTRANSMITTERS

The brain's inner workings are super technical, so rather than bore you with pages of complicated terms, I'll simplify it as much as possible without losing the overall meaning. Our brain is full of neurons located in different regions of the brain. Each region is responsible for different things, including some that regulate sleep.

Information in the neurons travels to and is shared with other regions in the brain thanks to neurotransmitters. ADHD was the first disorder found to be the result of a deficiency of a specific neurotransmitter, norepinephrine. It was also the first disorder found to respond positively to medications administered to correct this deficiency (Silver, 2022). Neurotransmitters play a role in both ADHD and the regulation of sleep. When they are not working as they should, we say they are *dysregulated*. Neurotransmitters such as dopamine, norepinephrine, and serotonin play crucial roles in regulating sleep-wake cycles. Dysregulation of these neurotransmitters can lead to difficulties falling asleep and maintaining sleep (Shen et al., 2020).

Scientists believe ADHD may involve impaired neurotransmitter activity in four functional regions of the brain:

1. **The frontal cortex,** responsible for high-level functioning.

2. **The limbic system,** which regulates our emotions.

3. **The basal ganglia,** which regulate communication within the brain.

4. **The reticular activating system,** the way many pathways enter and leave the brain (Silver, 2022).

We will delve a bit deeper into these four brain regions in the section on behavior.

Brain Structure and Function

If you have ever thought that your brain is just built differently, you're not entirely wrong. Research shows that the brains of individuals with ADHD have structural differences from the brains of those without. The amygdala and hippocampus are smaller in ADHD brains. These two areas are partly responsible for emotional regulation and impulsivity, affecting one's ability to control them.

During sleep, the amygdala is "reset," so to speak, so that tomorrow is not affected by today's emotions. Lack of sleep stops that process from happening properly, leading to more difficulty managing emotions. The hippocampus helps consolidate memories and is believed also to help improve our learning ability. More research is needed to better understand the implications of a smaller amygdala and hippocampus in ADHD brains (Goldstein & Walker, 2014).

There is also decreased blood flow to certain areas of the brain, including the prefrontal regions. The ADHD brain matures on average 1 to 3 years slower than a non-ADHD one, which is why children and teens can sometimes be accused of acting younger than their biological age. Some areas of the brain never achieve the same level of maturity as a non-ADHD brain (Sinfield, 2022). What this means for the impact on sleep is still an emerging field.

Behavioral Factors

We cannot control how our brains are wired, but unconscious neurobiological forces aren't always affecting our sleep. Our behaviors play a role in the quality of our sleep as well. Only with ADHD do those differences in our brains impact how we behave, meaning that we need to try to modify our behavior to be more conducive to getting a good night's sleep.

Earlier in the chapter, we discussed how differences in the ADHD brain involve impaired neurotransmitter activity in four functional regions of the brain, including the frontal cortex, the limbic system, the basal ganglia, and the reticular activating system. Dysregulation in these areas can have an impact on our behavior. Let's look more closely at each.

1. **The frontal cortex is responsible for high-level functioning.** Norepinephrine deficiency in this brain area can lead to problems with attention, organization, and executive functioning. Executive functioning involves skills like being able to plan ahead. Leaving too much to do in the hours before bed or being unable to organize your time to get to bed at a reasonable hour can lead to insufficient sleep. Repeated night after night, sleep deprivation can become a chronic problem.

2. **The limbic system regulates our emotions.** A deficiency in this region can make us restless, emotionally unstable, or inattentive. Inattention can show up as not realizing that time is flying and you should have been asleep hours ago. Restlessness can lead to avoiding bed or getting up in the middle of the night because your brain just won't turn off, and you have to do *something*.

3. **The basal ganglia regulate communication within the brain.** Deficiencies in this area can result in information not being delivered as it should. This can lead to attention problems and impulsivity. Have you suddenly had an urge to order a pizza at midnight? Or start a movie 20 minutes before you should be heading to bed? The inability to control impulses can be bad news for sleep.

4. **The reticular activating system is how many pathways enter and leave the brain.** Deficiency can cause inattention, impulsivity, and hyperactivity. Nobody wants to sleep when their energy levels are through the roof. Add in some impulsive urges, and sleep takes a backseat (Silver, 2022).

On the other hand, some behaviors stem from a lack of understanding of how to work around the challenges our brains pose.

- ☐ *Not having a set bedtime.* If you go to bed whenever you feel like it, your body may never send you the signals you're waiting for rather than having a set bedtime. Too much stimulation, hyperactivity, and inattention can make it difficult to know when to hit the sheets instinctively.

- ☐ *Not having a bedtime routine.* Similarly, not having a consistent set of actions you take before bed to signal that it's almost time to sleep can mean that your brain doesn't have the chance to register your intentions. Most kids have a routine of brushing their teeth, washing their face, using the toilet, putting on pajamas, and maybe a bedtime story before lights out. If you have lost that over the years, it's hard for your brain and body to take the hint when you are finally ready for sleep.

☐ *Participating in hyper-focused activities in the evening.* If you know that once you start putting together a puzzle, streaming a show, or reading a book, you will find it hard to stop, try not to schedule these activities at night. Or, set a timer to remind you to stop. Tasks and pastimes that don't overstimulate your brain or cause you to hyperfocus are better nighttime activities.

☐ *Eating and drinking too close to bedtime.* This goes along with organization and scheduling. Eating too close to bedtime can cause sleep disruptions, particularly consuming greasy, sugary, or heavy foods. Caffeine and alcohol also negatively affect sleep.

☐ *Not turning off electronics.* Playing video games, streaming shows, or even mindlessly scrolling until you try to sleep is counterproductive. The blue light emitted from screens can activate the brain, making you feel even more wired. It can be frustrating to lie in bed, unable to sleep, but picking up your phone to pass the time will just make things worse.

Chapter 4 will explore how to incorporate positive sleep habits into a nightly sleep routine.

Medication Factors

Not everyone with ADHD takes medication for it, but millions of people do, and the most common types are stimulants.

STIMULANTS

Stimulants increase the levels of certain neurotransmitters in the brain, specifically dopamine and norepinephrine. They fall into Amphetamines (such as Adderall) and Methylphenidates (such as Ritalin or Concerta). For the ADHD brain, stimulants have a calming effect, allowing for better focus. They come in both short- and long-acting formulations. However, they are also controlled substances and can come with serious side effects, including increased blood pressure, heart rate, body temperature, hostility and paranoia, decreased appetite, and sleep problems (National Institute on Drug Abuse, 2014). Insomnia, in particular, is a common side effect, no matter the formulation.

Stimulant medications are controlled substances because they are sometimes abused, being crushed and snorted. Stimulants are often misused for weight loss, to stay awake for long periods when working or studying, or to experience a sense of "euphoria" in individuals without ADHD. They are considered safe when prescribed in the correct doses and taken as prescribed. Still, it is important to be aware of the potential adverse side effects when not taken as prescribed (National Institute on Drug Abuse, 2014).

A study showed that 30% of children who take stimulant ADHD medication experience insomnia versus only 10% of children with ADHD who do not take it. (Stein, 2023). The connection is strong enough that as dosage increases, so does the rate of sleep disturbance. When the medication dose is at 18 mg, 8.5% of patients report sleep disturbances. The number rises to 11% at a 36 mg dose and jumps to 25% when the dose is at 54 mg (Stein, 2023). It seems counterintuitive that a stimulant that can calm your brain during the day can have the opposite effect at night, but it does.

NON-STIMULANTS

Non-stimulant medications are not as common but have been shown to be effective in treating ADHD symptoms in children and adults. Approximately 15-30% of individuals who try stimulants don't respond well to them, while others cannot tolerate the side effects. For people with a history of substance abuse, stimulants may not be recommended as an option at all (Miller, 2023). One of the benefits of some non-stimulants is that their effectiveness can last up to 24 hours, and they are not habit-forming.

Non-stimulant medications fall into two categories: Norepinephrine modulators, SNRIs, Selective Norepinephrine Reuptake Inhibitors, and Alpha Agonists.

1. **SNRIs:** These medications block the mechanism that removes norepinephrine, facilitating better signaling in the brain. While stimulants work immediately, non-stimulants can take up to six weeks to reach their full effect, and patients are often started on a low dose and then work their way up to avoid side effects such as stomachaches, headaches, and fatigue. Insomnia is reported in the initial adaptation phase but is not a long-term side effect (Miller, 2023).

2. **Alpha Agonists:** Unlike SNRIs that block the removal of norepinephrine, these medications stimulate receptors to release more of it. They are known to improve concentration while reducing hyperactivity and impulsivity. Like SNRIs, it takes time to reach maximum effectiveness, typically between 2 to 4 weeks. Loss of appetite, headache, dizziness, and fatigue are common side effects. These medications come in short- and long-acting formulations (Miller, 2023).

Perhaps the best news about all these medications is that they don't have to be either/or. Stimulant and non-stimulant medications do not interact negatively, so combining them to get the best of both worlds is possible. Some practitioners prescribe stimulant medications in the morning and then have patients switch to a non-stimulant in the afternoons or early evening.

Non-stimulant medications are used to treat sleep disturbances linked to stimulant use. One study showed that stimulant ADHD medication causes a 40-minute delay in the onset of sleep, while non-stimulants actually sped up the onset by 12 minutes (Stein, 2023). This is great news for those who struggle to fall asleep quickly.

ADHD and sleep are a complicated pair and inextricably linked. Treating one does not always help with the other, although non-stimulant medications seem to be reasonably effective at both.

So, what can you do to help improve your sleep besides taking medication? Chapter 4 will help you cultivate good sleep hygiene, a fancy way of saying that you will learn the good habits to adopt to get a better night's sleep.

Sleep Hygiene for ADHDers

Sleep hygiene refers to the actions and routines established to help set the stage for a restful night's sleep. It is specifically the behaviors we can control to make it more likely we can fall asleep and stay asleep the whole night through. In Chapter 3, we learned how differences in the brain can influence our behaviors in ways that make sleep difficulties more likely.

Knowledge is power, and knowing how the ADHD brain makes it harder to get a good night's sleep gives us the knowledge needed to formulate a plan of attack. Some sleep hygiene tips can be applied to anyone with sleep trouble, while others are more specific to the ADHD brain. Don't worry about putting them all in place at once. Choose one or two that seem most relevant to your specific situation and try them out for a few weeks to see if you notice any changes for the better. Then, you can add in other habits as needed.

Sleep Hygiene Begins As Soon As You Wake Up

Waking up groggy, tired, and cranky can set the stage for a bad day ahead. Daytime sleepiness, as we learned earlier, also affects a higher number of people with ADHD. Circadian rhythm problems can lead to people not feeling tired at night and feeling overly tired during the day.

THE CIRCADIAN CLOCK

The circadian clock is our internal guide to knowing when to feel tired and go to sleep and when to wake up and feel energetic. Setting yourself up for sleep at night begins with calibrating your circadian clock in the morning. In the time before modern technology, such as electricity, people woke up when the sun rose and went to sleep pretty soon after it got dark at night. Our bodies evolved to be sensitive to the light and dark cycle, except artificial light often disrupts that natural rhythm.

The circadian clock is most sensitive at three different times during the day.

1. **Within an hour of waking up in the morning:** The single most important element for setting our circadian clock is morning light (Marshall, 2022). Even 15 minutes a day is beneficial. Direct morning light impacts the body in a few different ways. First, it signals the brain to stop producing melatonin, the sleep hormone, so you can be awake and alert for the day ahead. It signals to the body that it should start producing cortisol to energize you for what lies ahead. Finally, your internal clock sets a timer to start producing melatonin again roughly 14 hours after the first exposure to light so that you will be ready to sleep through the night.

    All this happens within the first 60 minutes of waking up.

    What to do: Ideally, get outside within an hour of waking for a minimum of 15-30 minutes to benefit from natural light exposure. Standing beside a brightly lit window is an acceptable substitute, particularly when the weather isn't great. Living in a country with long, dark winters can be a challenge. Light therapy lamps, which mimic the light needed to reset our internal clocks,

are available for purchase and can be used daily during those
dark months.

Sitting next to windows during the day is also recommended to
get natural light on your face. Finally, taking another outdoor
walk between 1:00 and 3:00 pm, when the body tends to release
another spike of melatonin, can help fend off afternoon crashes
and keep us alert for the rest of the day (Marshall, 2022).

2. **One to two hours before normal bedtime:** In this case, your body
   should be getting less light to signal that it is time to wind down
   and relax for sleep. Note that it says, "before normal bedtime."
   This is the first problem for many people with ADHD who
   struggle to maintain a regular bedtime. Your body and brain rely
   on that routine to know when to signal that it's time to rest. If
   you don't have a regular bedtime and you are not introducing
   lower light environments, there is no way for the body to be able
   to start the sleep process effectively (Cooper, n.d.).

During the two hours before bed, the body requires less bright
light. Bright light exposure in the evening before bed can suppress
melatonin production, the hormone that helps us fall asleep.
Studies have found that the average household has artificial light
(lamps, overhead lights, etc.) bright enough to suppress melatonin
production by up to 50% (Cain et al., 2020). If you spend all of
your evening hours in a brightly lit home, it is more difficult for
your body to go through the necessary biological processes to set
you up for a full night's sleep.

Light from tablets, computers, and cell phones also plays a role in
keeping us awake. Aside from the distracting nature of those
devices that can cause us to lose track of time, their blue light
stimulates the brain. This can make it harder to fall asleep.

Consider removing them from the bedroom entirely to avoid temptation or putting them on Do not disturb overnight.

What to do: Dim the lights in the home in the evenings or use fewer of them. Soft light is better for relaxing the body and mind. Limit the use of devices such as phones and tablets, and stop using them an hour before you want to go to bed. Choose a non-tech activity instead. Use blue/green wavelength-blocking glasses in the evenings.

3. **Overnight:** Nights used to be dark. Light pollution is so intense that it never gets dark in some places, particularly urban areas. It doesn't take very much light to signal to the brain that it's time to wake up, and if light is constantly streaming in from outside, your brain may struggle to stay asleep.

    What to do: If you can afford room darkening or blackout curtains, they are worth the splurge. Just don't forget to open them first thing in the morning when you wake up for that hit of natural light. Sleep masks are also a good option, particularly if you have a partner who wants to stay up with the lights and screens on when you're trying to sleep.

    Exercise: Getting adequate exercise during the day can help you sleep better at night. Though some people enjoy going to the gym after work, if you have trouble sleeping at night, try to keep vigorous exercise to at least 5 or 6 hours before bedtime to avoid being too overstimulated to sleep.

    Food and Drink: Try to eat dinner at least three hours before bed to allow food to digest and not weigh you down. Caffeine or sugary drinks should be avoided after lunch as they may affect the ability to fall asleep.

Sleep Hygiene Habits for the Evening

1. **Schedule sleep and wake times:** This should become a priority if you don't have a set time to go to bed and wake up. Ideally, you should go to bed and wake up at the same time every day, including weekends and vacations. Our bodies like consistency, and going to bed and waking up at the same time helps the body and brain get into a routine, making it easier to go to sleep at night and wake up refreshed.

2. **Manage your environment:** Is your bedroom a place of rest? Or is it full of clutter and mess, or is it simply a multi-purpose room where you work, hang out, and try to sleep occasionally? How about your bed? Is it comfortable? Are the sheets clean? Is it inviting? Spend some time making the place you sleep conducive to sleep.

3. **White Noise:** This one is hit or miss, depending on the person, but for many people with ADHD, white noise, such as the noise of a fan, can help drown out other noises that would otherwise be distracting and make falling asleep difficult. If you live somewhere with a lot of noise you can't control, like a busy street, white noise can also help prevent it from waking you up during the night.

    If a fan doesn't sound like the thing for you, natural sounds such as rain or the ocean, classical music, or even ASMR (Autonomous Sensory Meridian Response) audio might work. I suggest you experiment until you find what's right for you. There are many, many sleep apps available for phones that provide numerous sounds that may help one fall asleep. Personally, I use Sleep Cycle - Sleep Tracker. It has all kinds of restful sounds and tracks my sleep cycles and quality. I've found it a very helpful tool to gauge how well I'm meeting my nightly sleep goals.

4. **Relaxation:** If our minds and bodies are unable to calm themselves down, it's not a bad idea to look for outside help. Below are some relaxation activities that may help induce sleep:

    ☐ *Yoga*, particularly gentle yoga, can relax the body and loosen tight, cramped muscles. Physically letting go of stress can help the mind follow. Stretching is a good option if following a yoga program isn't your thing.

    ☐ *Meditation or mindfulness*. Meditation doesn't have to involve chanting or sitting still for an hour. Guided meditations for relaxation and sleep are created to have a voice slowly guide you through relaxing different areas of the body and teach you how to quiet the mind. Mindfulness can be as simple as sitting quietly and practicing deep breathing to calm the body and mind. I often use an app called Insight Timer for guided yoga nidra relaxation meditations when I lie down to sleep.

5. **Self-Care:** When we slow down and focus on ourselves, it's easier to tune out distractions. Taking a warm bath, making a cup of nighttime tea, or even spending some time on an evening skincare routine may sound simple, but they turn our attention inwards and help signal that it's time to let go of the day.

6. **"Sleepy teas," bedtime teas, or herbal infusions:** These have natural relaxation qualities or can even induce sleep. They are not teas with caffeine but rather blends of herbs and plants that can help with sleep. The ritual of preparing and drinking the tea can help signal to the brain that it is time to relax. Consider making nighttime teas around one hour before bed in a calm environment. Allow the ritual to be part of your sleep routine.

Here are some teas that can help you sleep:

☐ *Lavender tea:* A natural relaxant that can help calm your nerves, reduce anxiety, and help you get a good night's sleep.

☐ *Chamomile tea:* A classic pre-bed drink known for reducing anxiety, soothing the nervous system, and regulating dopamine and serotonin.

☐ *Peppermint or spearmint tea:* Although mint is often associated with energy, peppermint and spearmint can help with digestion and promote relaxation.

☐ *Lemon balm tea:* Contains compounds that promote sleep and are thought to alleviate symptoms of depression and anxiety.

☐ *Passionflower tea:* Can help you fall asleep by promoting relaxation, calming restlessness, and reducing anxiety.

☐ *Melatonin tea:* Can help you fall asleep.

☐ *Kava tea:* A Polynesian tea known for aiding relaxation and treating sleeplessness.

☐ *Valerian root tea:* Has a long history of being used as a sleep and stress aid (Falcone, 2023).

7. **Journaling:** If you don't keep a journal but find your mind racing at night, you might want to start. Getting your thoughts out of your head, in a figurative sense, can help you to let them go before bed. Keeping a small notebook and pen by your bedside table can give you peace of mind that if you wake up at night with a thought you don't want to forget, there is somewhere to write it down so you can go back to sleep rather than stay up all night worrying that you will forget it by morning. I regularly write in my journal before bedtime as part of my nightly routine.

8. **Avoid activities that cause you to hyperfocus:** This was mentioned in Chapter 3, but it bears repeating. You know which activities put you at risk of hyperfocus, causing you to lose track of time, feel energized, and have trouble putting down. Don't participate in those activities for 2 or 3 hours before bedtime. If your body and brain are overstimulated, and you are going to have trouble shifting from that activity to winding down for bed, you aren't going to be able to fall asleep.

9. **Don't make insomnia or nighttime waking worse:** You can't always control whether your brain will be able to slow down long enough to let you sleep or whether something will cause you to wake up in the middle of the night. Rather than stubbornly lying in bed, trying your hardest to sleep, it might be more helpful to try and take your mind off sleep entirely. Getting up to do something may actually work to help you fall back asleep. It takes the anxiety and pressure of falling back asleep off your shoulders to start. The key is to choose your activity wisely. Perhaps reading a few pages of a book (if that isn't a hyperfocus activity for you), having a cup of warm nighttime tea, or doing a few pieces of a puzzle will help you relax enough to go back to bed and fall back asleep.

Yoga Nidra

Yoga nidra, also known as yogic sleep, is a meditation technique that offers numerous benefits, including helping with sleep problems. Unlike some demanding yoga practices, Yoga Nidra is incredibly accessible and suitable for all ages. This practice guides you through the five layers of self while you rest comfortably in savasana (corpse pose), ultimately leaving you with a profound sense of wholeness.

THE FIVE LAYERS OF SELF

1. **Physical:** This is, quite literally, your body. Being aware of how you feel, areas that feel tight or are in pain, and learning to relax your body are all components of this layer.

2. **Energy:** This layer is often accessed through breathwork, which can be used to increase or decrease energy and body temperature.

3. **Mental/Emotional:** This layer deals with our feelings and emotions and how they affect our physical state.

4. **Higher Intelligence:** Sometimes referred to as the wisdom body or intuition, this is when you may have insights or information that surprise you. It is often accessed during yoga nidra via the use of visualization.

5. **Bliss:** This is total absorption into a blissful state, typically observed in silence at the end of practice. When used as an exercise to promote sleep, it is very common to be able to fall into deep sleep from this state (Jeraci, n.d.a).

FIVE REASONS TO INCORPORATE YOGA NIDRA INTO YOUR NIGHTLY ROUTINE

1. **It suits all ages and abilities.** Unlike yoga, which moves through physical poses, yoga nidra is performed lying down or seated and follows a guided meditation. These meditations are available on apps or even YouTube for different ages, including for children.

2. **It is foolproof.** You listen to a guided meditation, so there's really nothing you can do wrong.

3. **It can be integrated easily into everyday life.** All you need is to access a guided meditation, find a calm spot, and listen to it. Use headphones to avoid external distractions.

4. **Self-Exploration.** It provides a safe space for exploring the inner self. You can work through long-held emotions and energy blocks, all from the comfort of your bed.

5. **Stress-Reduction.** Yoga nidra's effects go beyond simple meditation to calm the nervous system and improve overall well-being (Jeraci, n.d.b).

Lily, the college student from Chapter 3, decided to make some changes to her lifestyle to try to improve her sleep. Rather than running on the treadmill at the gym in the morning, she runs outside to get some sunshine first thing in the morning. She cut out snacking after 8 pm, opting instead for a cup of nighttime tea. The hardest habit to break was late-night scrolling on social media. To avoid temptation, Lily now turns off screens while having her evening tea and then chooses relaxation activities such as yoga nidra, meditation, or journaling before bed.

Although Lily can't quite bring herself to give up late nights on the weekend, she makes a point of keeping the same bedtime Sunday night through Thursday evening, saving only Friday and Saturday for going out and staying up late. In the space of one month, Lily's sleep has improved dramatically. She can fall asleep before midnight and has only been experiencing restless leg syndrome on average once a week. She no longer forgets her course material and does not struggle to stay awake in class. Now that her sleep problems are diminishing, she is motivated to keep moving forward and has an appointment with her family doctor to discuss the next steps.

If you have struggled with sleep for what seems like your entire life, know that the problem isn't going to be fixed overnight. However, creating and following good sleep hygiene can make it more likely that you will be able to improve the quality and quantity of your sleep.

Sometimes, behavior alone isn't enough to solve the problem. In Chapter 5, we will look at the supplements and prescription medications that can help make sleep disruption a thing of the past.

CHAPTER 5

Treating Sleep Problems with Medication

"Even if you're on medication, you still have to treat your body properly and take care of yourself. The idea that ADHD goes away, or you grow out of it isn't true."

—widely attributed to Ty Pennington

Sleep problems are not unique to ADHDers, but as we've already discussed, they do tend to not only be more common but also more complicated. The reciprocal influence of sleep deprivation on ADHD attributes and vice versa means that treating these issues is not always straightforward. It can sometimes feel like a losing battle, but fortunately, there have been many advancements in treatment options that are giving many people their full night's rest back.

A sleep study is recommended before taking any medication, either over-the-counter or prescription. Many people with ADHD have what is called *co-morbid* conditions, meaning something else that is contributing to certain symptoms, and the treatments for those conditions may address your sleep concerns. Sleep apnea is one such condition and is usually treated via weight loss, a CPAP machine and mask, or surgery. In cases of sleep apnea, medication isn't even in the top three treatment approaches.

Dealing with any underlying issues first can ensure that if and when you do begin medication, it is to deal specifically with the sleep issue at hand and won't mask something else. If you grew up with undiagnosed ADHD and were labeled everything from lazy to distracted or even a problem child, you understand how vital a proper diagnosis is. It's worth the extra time and effort to get it right.

You may wish to skip to Chapter 6 if you know medication isn't for you.

First Steps

Many people begin with their own ADHD medication to see if the problem can be solved without additional interventions.

1. **Reducing daytime stimulant medication dose:** For some patients, the long-lasting nature of some stimulant medications can cause sleep disturbance. Reducing the dose is often enough to reduce some nighttime sleep disturbance, mainly related to being able to fall asleep.

2. **Switching formulations:** Simply changing to a shorter-lasting formulation may help. Or, consider taking a higher dose of a shorter-acting medication in the morning, followed by a smaller dose of the same medication in the afternoon. This may allow individuals to have a higher dose during the daytime hours that typically require the most focus, such as school or work, and then taper it off in the late afternoon or evening without the typical crash that sometimes accompanies fast-acting formulations.

3. **Taking a stimulant before bed:** What? I had to read the research more than once to believe what I was reading. If restlessness caused by ADHD is what is causing difficulty when trying to fall asleep, sometimes taking a second dose of stimulant medication, the same kind you take during the day, can calm the restlessness

enough to fall asleep. One doctor said that approximately two-thirds of their adult patients take a full dose of their stimulant ADHD medication nightly before bed (Dodson, 2023).

4. **Taking a non-stimulant medication:** Confused yet? I was. The advice seems contradictory. On the one hand, taking a stimulant before bed can help. On the other hand, taking a non-stimulant is thought to be helpful. The truth is, there is no one magic pill that works for everyone. ADHD affects everyone differently, so the treatment approach must be individualized as well.

We covered non-stimulant medications in detail in Chapter 3, but to recap, non-stimulant medications are non-habit-forming formulations that are used to treat unwanted symptoms of ADHD. Some formulations have a 24-hour efficacy period, and they are safe to take with stimulants. The downside is that with some formulations, insomnia has been reported as a side effect during the adaptation phase. Still, they have successfully been used to treat sleep problems in individuals with ADHD.

Over-the-Counter Sleep Medications

Over-the-counter medications are those that can be sold at a pharmacy without the need for a prescription. Unlike prescription medications that can sometimes be intended for long-term use, these are intended for intermittent use only, meaning for the occasional sleepless night.

SOME PRECAUTIONS

☐ Even though they are available without a prescription, you should always consult your doctor before taking sleep medication in case of potential risk for an adverse reaction based on your medical history.

- [ ] Never mix sleep medication with alcohol or illegal drugs. Ensure that your medications are not contraindicated, meaning they shouldn't mix.

- [ ] Do not drive or operate heavy machinery.

- [ ] Take far enough in advance to be able to dedicate a full 8 hours to sleep. For some people, the effects can last even longer, and people often wake up groggy.

- [ ] Follow the dosage on the package and remember that non-prescription sleep aids are not meant for long-term use. Many contain histamines as the active ingredient to induce sleep, something the body gets accustomed to over time, making the medication less effective.

- [ ] Some medications are not recommended for people with certain health conditions, including glaucoma, ulcers, pregnancy, or while breastfeeding, and might pose risks for people over age 65, including an increased risk of dementia. (Mayo Clinic Staff, 2022a) Again, always thoroughly read medication labels, including directions and precautions, before taking anything.

1. DIPHENHYDRAMINE

For patients without restlessness and agitation as the primary difficulty in falling asleep, a drowsy formulation of Benadryl or other antihistamine is sometimes recommended. Robitussin and Sudafed are other brand names with the same active ingredient. It allows the brain to relax, is not prescription grade, nor is it habit forming. A word of caution, however. Up to 10% of patients experience the opposite effect with medications that typically cause drowsiness and experience hyperactivity instead (Dodson, 2023).

In healthy people under 65, dry mouth and dizziness have been known to occur. In older adults, the anticholinergic properties can cause confusion, hallucinations, dry mouth, blurred vision, constipation, nausea, impaired sweating, urinary retention, and rapid heart rate (tachycardia) (Mayo Clinic Staff, 2022b).

2. DOXYLAMINE

ZzzQuil and Unisom Sleep Tabs are brand-name sleep meds that use Doxylamine as an active ingredient. They are antihistamines that are also used to treat insomnia. For insomnia, these are usually available in tablet form for children and adults ages 12 and up. The side effects are generally considered to be similar to Diphenhydramine, except that it tends to stay in your system longer, which can result in more next-day drowsiness. It is also why the dosage for products with this active ingredient is typically lower.

It should be used with caution when given at the same time as central nervous system depressant drugs. Doxylamine contraindications include patients with elevated intraocular pressure, glaucoma, asthma, ulcers, urinary bladder neck obstruction, and gastric outlet obstruction (Brott & Reddivari, 2019).

3. MELATONIN

Melatonin is not a medication but rather a hormone that your brain produces naturally in the pineal gland. It helps to regulate your circadian rhythm and is released in preparation for sleep. Melatonin levels increase approximately two hours before bedtime to help you feel drowsy and ease the transition to sleep. However, it is common for those with ADHD to still have insufficient melatonin production. On top of that, the older you get, the less melatonin you produce, whether you have ADHD or not. Fortunately, it can be taken in synthetic pill form.

Before taking synthetic melatonin, there are things you can do to support natural melatonin production. Earlier, we discussed the importance of sunlight exposure shortly after waking to help regulate melatonin production at the right time to ensure a good sleep-wake cycle. Sleeping in anything other than complete darkness can decrease melatonin production, throwing off your body clock. The blue light emitted from screens and tablets can also suppress melatonin production. Finally, consider a magnesium supplement. Magnesium helps with the production of melatonin and also works as a natural sleep aid (Higuera, 2022).

If the above activities don't result in better sleep, taking synthetic melatonin before bed can help make falling asleep easier for some people. In addition, it can help you fall into a deeper sleep, reducing the number and frequency of sleep interruptions during the night. Unlike sleeping pills that work relatively quickly, melatonin takes longer to be effective. Melatonin signals to the brain that it is time to prepare the body for sleep, and then the brain needs to do its thing. All of this takes time. For that reason, it is best taken 1 to 2 hours before bedtime (Pederson, 2023). Supplements come in a variety of forms, including pills, sprays, and gummies.

POTENTIAL BENEFITS

In addition to helping people get better sleep, there are some potential benefits associated with melatonin use.

- ☐ May have therapeutic anticancer effects, protecting against several cancers.

- ☐ Boosts the immune system.

- ☐ May reduce the risk of Alzheimer's disease.

- ☐ May slow the progression of ALS disease.

- ☐ Reduces blood pressure in males with untreated hypertension.

- ☐ May reduce the pain associated with irritable bowel syndrome.

- ☐ May enhance the effectiveness of invitro-fertilization treatments.

- ☐ May reduce the severity of COVID-19 symptoms (Higuera, 2022).

POSSIBLE SIDE EFFECTS

- ☐ The long-term effects have not been well-researched.

- ☐ May interact with certain medications, so consult with a doctor before use.

- ☐ May cause irritability, drowsiness, headache, nausea, and diarrhea.

- ☐ It is possible to overdose on melatonin, which can be dangerous.

- ☐ Too much melatonin can cause rebound insomnia or an increased risk of sleep inertia (Higuera, 2022).

Prescription Medications

Prescription sleep medications are formulated differently from over-the-counter ones and are more potent. They are formulated to help you fall asleep faster, stay asleep longer, or both. Often, doctors will recommend these if other methods have been unsuccessful or if there is an exceptional reason for sleeplessness, such as a traumatic event.

You may hear them referred to as hypnotics, sedatives, sleep aids, sleep medicine, or even tranquilizers.

This class of medication requires a prescription because they can often be habit-forming, making your body dependent on them for sleep. If you are taking these meds for an extended period and then stop suddenly, you can experience intense symptoms, including something called rebound insomnia, where your insomnia returns worse than it was before you started taking the pills. Your doctor should be your partner in the decision to stop taking sleeping pills because it can sometimes take months to wean your body off them in a way that avoids the worst of the after-effects.

Different formulations have various potential side effects that we will discuss below. Still, some of the most commonly shared ones include:

- ☐ Drowsiness, dizziness, and balance problems the next day, known as the hangover effect. Up to 8 out of 10 people report experiencing these side effects in particular.

- ☐ Constipation or diarrhea

- ☐ Dry mouth

- ☐ Headache

- ☐ Muscle weakness

- ☐ Gas, heartburn, and nausea (digestive problems) (Cleveland Clinic, 2021a).

There are distinct classes of prescription sleep medication.

ANTIDEPRESSANTS

Are you surprised? Antidepressants are typically used to treat depression, anxiety, and stress. For some people, any of those is enough to cause sleep dysregulation. The way that sedating antidepressants work in general is by influencing the neurotransmitters in the central nervous system to promote relaxation and sleep, so even if it is not depression or anxiety causing your sleeplessness, these medications can still potentially help. Amitriptyline, Mirtazapine, and Trazodone are examples.

Antidepressants can have serious side effects, so it's important to report anything concerning to your doctor. Irregular heartbeat, memory problems, weight gain, and suicidal thoughts are all potential side effects. Do not just stop taking an antidepressant. Speak with your doctor and follow their advice.

BENZODIAZEPINES (BENZOS)

This class of medication is a controlled substance, and for good reason. It is a highly addictive class of drugs, and the abuse of Benzos has serious consequences. When used properly under the care of a doctor, they can effectively treat several conditions, such as seizure disorders, anxiety, and mental health conditions. They are commonly prescribed by doctors to treat a number of conditions and have decades of research to back up their efficacy since they have been in use since the 1960s (Cleveland Clinic, 2023b).

These medicines tell your brain to release a neurotransmitter called gamma-aminobutyric acid (GABA), which makes your nervous system less active, affecting you in four different ways:

1. **Amnestic,** which temporarily blocks the formation of new memories.

2. **Anxiolytic,** which has the effect of lessening anxiety.

3. **Hypnotic,** which makes you sleepy.

4. **Sedative,** which has a quieting effect on your nervous system.

Depending on what condition is being treated, the strength and duration of the formulation may vary. Some brand names include Valium, Xanax, Restoril, Ativan, Lorazepam, Clonazepam, and Klonopin (Miller, 2023).

On the other hand, misuse of these drugs is rampant in the United States. Studies show that 17% of adults who have used them in the past report having misused them and that 35% of people who take them for more than 4 consecutive weeks will become dependent on them. They can combat sleep disorders but should not generally be considered a long-term solution (Miller, 2023).

Common side effects include:

- ☐ Drowsiness
- ☐ Light-headedness or confusion
- ☐ Dizziness
- ☐ Slurred speech
- ☐ Muscle weakness
- ☐ Memory problems
- ☐ Dry mouth
- ☐ Blurred vision

Less common side effects include:

- ☐ Low blood pressure
- ☐ Increased saliva production
- ☐ Digestive disturbances
- ☐ Rashes

- ☐ Tremors (shaking)
- ☐ Changes in sexual desire
- ☐ Incontinence (loss of bladder control) (Mind, 2021)

Nonbenzodiazepines, Also Known as Z-Class

Nonbenzodiazepines work in the body in a similar way to benzodiazepines, but they aren't exactly the same. For one thing, they produce fewer anxiolytic (anxiety-reducing) and anticonvulsant (seizure-reducing) effects than benzodiazepines and tend to be more fast-acting. They also have fewer side effects than benzodiazepines. They are almost always prescribed specifically as sleep aids and can help you get 8 hours of uninterrupted sleep. Some brands include Lunesta, Sonata, and Ambien. However, they are still just as habit-forming, so there continues to be a risk of misuse and dependency. The use of these drugs should be carefully monitored by a doctor, and you should be weaned off them following the doctor's directions (College of Physicians and Surgeons of Nova Scotia, 2023).

Long-term use of prescription sleep aids can have adverse effects on the brain and body. These drugs alter the brain in different ways. They come with the risk of dementia, memory problems, brain degeneration, Alzheimer's disease, depression, sexual dysfunction, and respiratory depression during sleep, which may lead to death. You may even experience parasomnia behaviors, such as talking in your sleep, sleepwalking, night terrors, sleep paralysis, or sleep-related eating disorders. Sometimes it can sound like the cure is worse than the illness.

None of this is to scare you from seeking help from pharmacological solutions as an option. These drugs are typically safe when used as prescribed but should be used under very specific circumstances and in the care of a doctor.

Choosing the Right Medication

Many doctors recommend that patients begin with non-pharmacological solutions, work up to non-prescription, and finally to prescription medications if needed. Choosing which options are not right for you can help narrow down your best choices.

If possible, start with a sleep study and a general check-up to rule out any possible medical reasons for your sleep troubles other than ADHD. Treating any underlying issues first ensures that you aren't just masking the problem with medication. Next, make sure you have a record of your medical history to discuss with your doctor. Some medicines are not to be used if the patient has certain conditions, which may exclude some options.

Next, take a look at the formulations, how long they last, and what the potential side effects are, and discuss which might be right for you with your doctor. Keeping a journal or jotting down how you feel and any side effects you may be experiencing once you try a medication can help you see if it is working or causing any concerning side effects that you might not recognize right away.

How to Stop Taking Prescription Sleep Medications

Unlike non-prescription medications, you should never just stop taking prescription drugs cold turkey. Since they are habit-forming, you can experience withdrawal symptoms if you don't wean them off slowly. Your best course of action is to talk to your doctor about your decision and then follow their recommended plan. Usually, this includes lowering the dose slowly until you don't take any at all. Your doctor will probably continue to monitor you for any withdrawal symptoms for a short period after that.

Tackling sleep issues with ADHD can be complicated, and there is no one quick fix. There are other treatment options that do not involve medication or can be used as a complement to meds. In Chapter 6, we will explore how cognitive behavioral therapy for sleep works and how you can incorporate it into your life to help improve the quality and quantity of your sleep.

CHAPTER 6

Cognitive-Behavioral Therapy for Sleep Problems

Whether you want to try a non-pharmacological approach to getting a better night's sleep or hope to use it as a complementary approach, Cognitive Behavioral Therapy for Insomnia (CBT-I or CBTI) is considered the most effective therapy currently available. It is effective for those with ADHD as well as for those without it.

What is Cognitive Behavioral Therapy for Insomnia (CBT-I)?

Cognitive behavioral therapy for insomnia (CBT-I) is a type of psychotherapy that aims to help people with chronic sleep problems improve their sleep quality and quantity. It can help improve the time it takes to fall asleep, help lessen the number of interruptions during the night, and increase overall sleep time and quality.

CBT-I is based on the idea that insomnia is maintained by cognitive and behavioral factors that interfere with the natural sleep process. It is so successful that it is currently recommended as the first-line treatment for chronic insomnia before any other interventions, including medication. As the name suggests, it is a combination of both cognitive therapy and behavioral therapy practices. It focuses on restructuring the thoughts, feelings, and behaviors contributing to a poor night of sleep.

Sessions are led by a trained medical professional such as a psychologist, psychiatrist, or medical doctor specializing in sleep disorders. The course of treatment itself tends to be short as far as therapy goes, typically between 4 to 6 sessions (Peters, 2019).

It is an effective and safe treatment for insomnia. It has been shown to improve both subjective and objective measures of sleep quality and quantity, as well as daytime functioning and mood. CBT-I can be practiced in individual or group settings or through self-help materials or online programs, so if going into an office for sessions doesn't work for you, you can still benefit from it.

CBT-I ADDRESSES THE FOLLOWING AREAS THAT TYPICALLY CONTRIBUTE TO PERSISTENT INSOMNIA.

There are several areas that can affect sleep. CBT-I can help identify some and actively work on others. Understanding the factors that apply to your situation can help you address them.

1. **Predisposing factors:** These variables can make you more likely to suffer from insomnia. Things like genetics, childhood experiences, and certain health conditions, including ADHD - as we already know, can increase your risk of developing chronic insomnia.

2. **Precipitating factors:** These can set off insomnia, which can persist even once the precipitating factor is gone. Things like a stressful or traumatic event, an illness, or an injury may trigger sleep issues that don't resolve.

3. **Conditioned arousal:** This is an area that CBT-I can actively address. Arousal, in this sense, refers to your body's general level of alertness. It changes during the day and can be influenced by several things, such as caffeine, exercise, mental stimulation, food, excitement, and more.

Conditioned arousal is learned over time. It's something you teach yourself. Let me explain. If you wake up to the aroma of coffee that your spouse makes for you each morning, your taste buds will anticipate that coffee every day, and you may even find yourself waking up roughly at the same time in anticipation. You have conditioned your body to create that level of arousal each morning. That's a positive example and can be used to condition yourself positively.

When it comes to insomnia, conditioned arousal isn't quite so positive. Rather than preparing your body to sleep, you have unintentionally conditioned it to stay awake even longer. Let's say you have been waking up each night between 1:00 am and 3:00 am and struggling to fall back asleep. Your morning alarm goes off at 6:30 am, and since you have a hard time falling asleep before midnight in the first place, these middle-of-the-night wake-up sessions are more than just an inconvenience; they set you up for a day of exhaustion ahead.

So, how do you react when you realize you've woken up *again* in the middle of the night? Maybe you decide you are not going to check the time. So you roll over, try to get comfortable, and think about falling back asleep. Then you eventually give in and check the time, mentally calculating how much sleep you can get if you fall asleep *right this second*. Which, of course, you can't. So now you're frustrated that you're awake. You are worried about how little sleep you're getting and how tired you will be the next day. So, instead of falling back asleep, you either toss and turn until dawn or pull out your phone and start scrolling, hoping it will make you tired.

The long-term effect of this is that over time, your body will begin expecting to wake up in the middle of the night, and you will get stressed out before you even go to bed, essentially creating the same cycle night after night. Cognitive behavioral therapy will help you break that pattern, and we will discuss how that works later in the chapter (Wu, n.d.).

4. **Habits developed to improve sleep but become ineffective over time:** This is another area where behavioral changes can help. People do many things to try to get better sleep, but not all of them are advisable. Other actions may work temporarily but may gradually lose effectiveness. Chapter 5 discussed over-the-counter sleep meds and how the body adapts to antihistamines over time, making them less effective. Similarly, behaviors that work temporarily, like staying up late to tire yourself out, may lose effectiveness over the long term. CBT-I will help identify these habits, break them, and replace them with more effective ones.

5. **Reducing sleep-related worry:** This specifically concerns your emotional state and how thinking and worrying about sleep can become a cycle that actually leads to worse sleep. While you can see elements of this in other sections above, this focuses on changing your mindset.

How It Works: CBT-I Interventions

COGNITIVE RESTRUCTURING

This technique involves challenging and replacing negative, incorrect, or unrealistic thoughts about sleep, such as "I can't function without eight hours of sleep" or "I will never overcome my insomnia." These thoughts can cause anxiety and frustration, which make it harder to fall asleep or stay asleep. How we think affects more than just our mental state. Our thoughts can affect our actions and our physical health.

Cognitive restructuring aims to break through the cycle by first identifying these thoughts because sometimes our thoughts are so automatic, we don't even notice them anymore. Next, you work to challenge these thoughts, which is perhaps the hardest part of this exercise. You may feel like you'll never get a full night's sleep again, but is that true? Is it true you're just not cut out to sleep more than 5 hours a night? Until you can successfully challenge your negative or incorrect thoughts, you can't move on to the last part of the restructuring process, which is replacing them with positive, healthy, and affirming thoughts.

Similar to how breaking a bad habit is easier when you have a good habit to replace it with, you must substitute the unhelpful thoughts with ones that are more balanced and positive about sleep, such as "I can cope with some sleep loss," or "I can improve my sleep habits" (Sleep Health Foundation, 2023).

STIMULUS CONTROL

This technique creates a strong, positive association between the bed and sleep. For many people, the bedroom is multi-purpose. You may have a desk or workspace, a television or entertainment center, a craft space, a yoga mat or weights, or other areas and activities that have little or nothing to do with sleep. On top of this, if you have been frustrated about your sleep difficulties for a long time, then the bedroom itself can bring up frustration or other negative emotions.

Stimulus control aims to change that. The bed is not to be used for anything other than sleep or sex during treatment. There is no reading, scrolling your phone, finishing up that work document, or anything else incompatible with improving your sleep.

Stimulus control also involves implementing good sleep hygiene habits, as discussed in Chapter 4. This includes following a regular sleep schedule, avoiding naps, and getting out of bed if unable to fall asleep within 20 minutes. These behaviors help to strengthen the body's natural sleep-wake cycle and reduce the arousal that can interfere with sleep.

SLEEP RESTRICTION AND COMPRESSION

1. **Sleep Restriction:** This technique aims to reduce the amount of time people with insomnia spend in bed without sleeping. Lying in bed, awake, unable to sleep, is unproductive and can lead to increasingly worse sleep. Sleep restriction is done by first calculating how many hours, on average, you actually sleep per night and then adding a small allowance of around 15 to 30 minutes to that. For example, if you typically go to bed at Midnight and wake up at 7 am but only sleep for 4 hours in between, you would be allowed to be in bed for 4.5 hours to lessen the time spent thinking about sleep. This technique also creates mild sleep deprivation, increasing the sleep drive and reducing the time spent awake in bed. As sleep improves, the time in bed gradually increases until a regular sleep schedule is achieved (Sleep Foundation, 2023).

2. **Sleep Compression:** This is a common technique used with older patients. Rather than drastically reducing the amount of time allowed in bed from the start, they gradually reduce it. If you go to bed at 10 p.m. and get up at 7 a.m., perhaps you would begin going to bed at 10:30 p.m. or getting up at 6:30 a.m. The effect is eventually the same, reducing the time you spend in bed without sleeping, but the approach is much gentler (Sleep Health Foundation, 2023).

PROGRESSIVE MUSCLE RELAXATION

Progressive muscle relaxation is a technique that involves slowly tensing and then releasing each muscle in your body to release tension and anxiety. It is best done while lying down; it's a great activity to help you drift off to sleep. While simple enough to do on your own, it is a good idea to use a guided relaxation audio the first few times until you can perform the entire exercise without having to think about it. There are many free videos available on sites like YouTube that are excellent for beginners. Studies have shown that progressive muscle relaxation is effective for treating insomnia. In fact, it's one of only three psychological treatments for insomnia backed by empirical evidence (Carefoot, 2023).

The process is simple: Lie down in a comfortable, quiet spot. Close your eyes and take a few calming breaths. Next, starting with your toes, tense the muscles in your toes and feet, holding the muscles tight for a count of ten before releasing them completely. Slowly work your way up your body, repeating the exercise with all the muscles of your body, moving from your feet to your head—end by tensing the muscles of your face, including your eyelids, before releasing into complete relaxation. The idea is to tighten and stress the muscles and then release all that tension and more when they relax.

HYPNOSIS

Hypnosis is a bit like being on the edge of sleep, and practitioners claim it helps individuals who have insomnia make the leap between wake and sleep more easily. Sleep hypnosis guided by a hypnotherapist is not designed to have you fall asleep during the session. Instead, it aims to help individuals change their future sleep habits by focusing on sleep during the session and is often used in conjunction with CBT-I.

Essentially, sleep hypnosis works by helping prepare your mind and, by extension, your body for sleep. Calming the mind means leaving behind the concerns of the day rather than anticipating what needs to be done tomorrow. When the mind is calm and not anxious or overwhelmed, it sends a message to the body that it is time to relax.

A sleep hypnotherapist helps this process by providing suggestions to your subconscious during the session about the benefits of a good night's sleep; this will help reset your internal sleep clock and help you get a better night's sleep. While anyone can try sleep hypnosis, not everyone can be hypnotized. Approximately 10% of people are very responsive to hypnosis, while another 10% are very resistant to it (Kim, 2022). However, with few negative reported side effects, it may be worth a try.

There are also many videos and apps out there that have guided hypnosis available to try at home. The quality of these videos varies, so you may have to try a few before finding one that works for you.

SELF-HYPNOSIS

If attending sessions by a professional hypnotherapist feels out of the question, you can always try self-hypnosis. While the goal is not necessarily to put yourself to sleep, practicing sleep hypnosis while in bed can be an easy way to associate relaxed feelings with where you are supposed to fall asleep.

Begin by focusing on your breath, bringing it to a slow and steady rhythm. Then, practice progressive relaxation, beginning either at the head or the feet, tensing and relaxing muscles in progression. Then, introduce a suggestion. Your suggestion is something you would like to adopt that will help improve your sleep, such as "I will sleep throughout the night" or "If I wake up before the alarm, I will simply close my eyes and go back to sleep." One sleep suggestion in a session is enough, especially at the beginning.

If you want to sleep immediately following a session, try falling asleep without regaining awareness of your surroundings. To return to a normal state, try counting to five while slowly regaining your conscious awareness. Like most exercises, practice is key. Give yourself a few weeks of practice to recognize any noticeable effect (Harley, 2020).

BIOFEEDBACK

In biofeedback therapy, individuals learn to control bodily processes that are usually autonomic- such as heart rate, blood pressure, and muscle tension. It is most effective in conditions typically brought on or worsened by stress. In a biofeedback session, electrodes are usually attached to the body, and they send information about various body processes to a monitor that displays them via a line on a grid—a visual measurement of brightness or a pitch that can be heard. A therapist guides the individual through a series of mental exercises, monitoring the changes in readings along the way. Through trial and error, they learn which exercises achieve the desired results.

Biofeedback is considered safe for children and adults but typically requires between 8 and 10 sessions to get results, and follow-up sessions may be needed. Eventually, the individual should be able to complete the exercises independently and experience the same beneficial results as when guided (Mount Sinai, n.d.).

AUTOGENIC TRAINING

Autogenic training was developed in the 1920s as a way to increase feelings of calm in your body to reduce feelings of anxiety or stress.

The goal is to gain control over the physical expressions of stress in the body. It is typically performed with a therapist in conjunction with other therapies but can be practiced alone or with a guided video. You use your mind to control your body.

Choose a comfortable spot and position, and begin focusing on slowing down your breathing. Tell yourself: "I am completely calm." Then, shift your focus to different parts of your body, indicating that the body part is heavy and you are completely calm. For example, "My right leg is heavy. I am completely calm." Then, shift your attention to your heartbeat, abdomen, chest, and the rest of your body. Your mind should relax, and anxiety should gradually subside as you do this. This can leave you calm and relaxed, with a steady heartbeat and less stress and anxiety than when you began. Hopefully, it may improve your sleep (Lindberg, 2019).

BREATHING EXERCISES

There are a myriad of breathing exercises designed for relaxation and sleep. In this book, we will just cover one simple but effective exercise called Box Breathing. A staple in meditation, Box Breathing is a wonderful technique for calming the body and mind, as your focus is on your breath and nothing else.

It's easy to start with this exercise: Sit up, breathe in, and then exhale, pushing all the air out of your lungs. Inhale slowly to a slow count of four, filling your lungs as much as possible. Hold your breath for a count of four, then exhale through your mouth, releasing all the air from your lungs. Repeat 10 or more times. You can also increase the count on the inhale and hold as you become more comfortable with the practice (Leavitt, 2022).

RELAXATION TRAINING

This encompasses a combination of exercises whose purpose is to relax the mind and body to allow it to be ready for sleep. There is no single technique used here, but rather a range of exercises that can be implemented to suit your needs. These exercises are fairly simple to learn and easy to incorporate into your daily routine. If an exercise is frustrating, too difficult, or impractical, it should be replaced with another. The goal is to induce relaxation, not stress.

Some common exercises incorporated into relaxation training include meditation and mindfulness exercises, and yoga nidra, all discussed in other chapters, as well as progressive muscle relaxation, guided or self-hypnosis, biofeedback, autogenic training, and breathing exercises.

SLEEP HYGIENE AND RELATED BEHAVIORS

As we covered in Chapter 4, sleep hygiene refers to the actions you take to increase the chances of getting a good night's sleep, like choosing the same sleep and wake time, having a dark, quiet room to sleep in, and avoiding caffeine, alcohol, or sugary drinks too close to bedtime. This part of CBT-I can also help people create a plan of what to do (or not to do) should they struggle to fall asleep or should they wake up during the night. One such suggestion is to never stay awake longer than 20 minutes in bed. It is better to get up and do something to take your mind off of not falling asleep than to lie in bed worrying about it.

HOMEWORK

This is the behavior part of cognitive-behavioral. This treatment option is, at its core, action-oriented. You have to put in the work to see the results, and since sleep isn't something you can do at the therapist's office nightly, you will need the motivation and discipline to implement the homework activities on your own, at home. Homework is really the make-it-or-break-it part of the therapy because, without it, it's all just theory (Sleep Health Foundation, 2023).

This sounds straightforward, but it's not always as easy as it seems. If you are confronting sleep issues due to trauma or past incidents, or if your home circumstances make it difficult or impossible to implement some of the suggestions, completing your homework may be difficult. Speak with your therapist and be open about your challenges so you can discover alternatives that work.

Cognitive Behavioral Therapy for Insomnia doesn't work perfectly for everyone, but it is a very successful approach to treating chronic insomnia. It is also compatible with other approaches, so combining it with other treatments is possible until you find the mix that works for you. In Chapter 7, we will delve into complementary and alternative therapies for sleep dysfunction, including some common supplements known for their sleep-inducing properties.

CHAPTER 7

Complementary and Alternative Medicine for Sleep Problems

*"Sometimes I've got too many thoughts at once. It's
like there's a four-way intersection in my brain where
everyone's trying to go at the same time."*

—widely attributed to A. J. Finn

If you can identify with the quote above, especially at night when you
should be winding down to sleep, you're not alone. Shutting your
brain off can be harder than relaxing your body sometimes. In the
last two chapters, we discussed the conventional approaches to
treating sleep disorders, including adjusting the use of ADHD
medication, over-the-counter medications, prescription medication
options, and cognitive behavioral therapy for insomnia.

Maybe the thought of changing up your medication schedule or
adding another medication to the list makes you uncomfortable, or
you have already tried everything previously mentioned. Perhaps
you're looking for some fresh ideas to treat sleep problems since
thinking outside the box is something you're already comfortable
doing. Whatever the reason, there is no shortage of complementary
and alternative treatment options to choose from.

Supplements

Many supplements are considered great for helping improve sleep, but be aware they are not Food and Drug Administration-approved in many cases. Their reputation often comes from anecdotal evidence, or they are traditional treatments in the United States or abroad. In some cases, it can be dangerous to mix a specific supplement with certain medications, or they are not recommended if you have a specific medical condition. Always read labels, research, and talk to your doctor before taking something new.

Five of the Most Common Supplements for Sleep

MELATONIN

Melatonin was mentioned in Chapter 5. It is known as the sleep hormone. Your body naturally produces it to help signal to your body that it's time to rest. The level of melatonin in your body should drop during the day with light exposure and rise at night when the sun goes down. A disruption in production, such as a result of jet lag, or for those of us with ADHD, can lead to sleep problems. Supplementing with melatonin 1-3 hours before bedtime is a common alternative to traditional sleeping pills.

Melatonin supplements are easy to find and are usually available for adults and children without a prescription. Studies have shown that supplementing with melatonin can shorten the time it takes to fall asleep, increasing overall sleep time. If you work night shifts and need to sleep during the day, it has been shown to be effective at helping with that as well (Suni & Rehman, 2023).

It is considered safe for short-term use for adults, but few studies have been done on long-term effects. It can sometimes cause minor side effects such as dizziness, headaches, and nausea. Melatonin comes in several forms, including pills, gummies, tabs, drops, and sprays. Doses come in anything from 1 mg to 10 mg doses. Speak to a pharmacist or doctor to determine your correct starting dose.

MAGNESIUM

Magnesium is a mineral everyone needs, but not everyone gets enough. It is involved in hundreds of actions in the body, and insufficient levels have been tied to sleep problems. Magnesium appears to increase levels of gamma-aminobutyric acid (GABA), a calming brain messenger we learned about in Chapter 5.

Magnesium is a natural alternative to pharmaceutical drugs that have the same effect on the brain. Magnesium also helps regulate melatonin production and has a relaxing effect on muscles, making it an all-around champ when it comes to helping body and mind relax and prepare for sleep.

Magnesium is available in several formats and is safe to combine with many other supplements to increase its effectiveness. For example, a combination of magnesium, melatonin, and vitamin B has been shown to be effective in treating insomnia. Some people experience diarrhea when taking magnesium, so start at a low dose to see how your body responds. High doses are associated with nausea and vomiting (Petre, 2023).

VALERIAN

Valerian is a sleep aid created using the root of a tall, flowering grassland plant. There are multiple valerian species, but most studies have been done on the Valeriana variety. Unlike melatonin or magnesium, valerian tends to improve sleep over time, not immediately. On average, it takes about two weeks of taking it nightly for best results, so be patient (Mayo Clinic Staff, 2022a).

Valerian has a reputation for inducing very vivid dreams, so don't be surprised if you start having some interesting ones shortly after you begin using it. However, for others, those dreams can come in the form of nightmares, negating any of the benefits of sleeping for extended periods. It is a common supplement for menopausal and postmenopausal women, so if you happen to have ADHD and also fit into one of these categories, it might be a good option for you.

Valerian root can cause some side effects other than bad dreams, the most concerning of which is heart palpitations. People have also reported experiencing nausea, diarrhea, and headaches. It can be problematic if mixed with some medications, so talk to your doctor before using.

CANNABIDIOL (CBD)

This one is a bit more controversial, partly because it isn't legal in all states, so make sure you aren't breaking any laws. Cannabidiol (CBD) is derived from hemp. Unlike THC, the active ingredient in marijuana, it doesn't cause a high and has been prescribed for a variety of health conditions in countries where it has been legal for many years. Some studies suggest that CBD may relieve anxiety and act as a natural sleep aid, potentially alleviating insomnia symptoms when used alone or with THC.

The endocannabinoid system regulates various bodily functions, including sleep. The word "cannabinoid," contained within the name of the system, refers to the active constituents of the cannabis sativa plant that impact the system. The compound CBD has been found to relax people and reduce pain. It may also improve sleep by ensuring that the body moves through the normal stages of sleep, including REM sleep, without too many interruptions. It has also been shown to act on another cause of sleep disruption: restless leg syndrome.

However, further high-quality research is needed to recommend CBD routinely for sleep disorders. It's essential to note that long-term safety and legal considerations for CBD use vary by location. It may be contraindicated for people taking statins, blood thinners, anti-inflammatories, and hypertension medications (McDermott, 2023).

GLYCINE

Glycine is an amino acid that plays a role in the nervous system and may help improve sleep. Taking glycine before sleep can improve overall sleep quality and reduce feelings of tiredness the next day. It is believed to work by lowering body temperature at bedtime, signaling the body that it's time to sleep. For those of us who are sleep-deprived, it may improve daytime performance. It is available in multiple formulations, including gelcaps, powders, and creams.

You can also increase glycine intake by consuming foods rich in this nutrient. Meat, including red meat, chicken, turkey, and pork, hard cheese, seeds, nuts such as peanuts or almonds, quinoa, beans and soybeans, bread, canned salmon, granola, pasta, and eggs are all high in glycine (Myrhe & Sifris, 2023).

Common side effects include nausea, vomiting, upset stomach, and diarrhea. Supplements can also interact with antipsychotic drugs, and overdose, while rare, can be fatal.

Aromatherapy

Many people swear by essential oils to remedy all sorts of ailments, and disordered sleep is no exception. While most people consider these oils harmless, it is important to use them only as directed. While some oils can be used topically, meaning directly on your skin, others can cause rashes. Similarly, some oils can cause unpleasant side effects if taken orally. Since they are unregulated, it is best to avoid ingestion. Always read and follow instructions before use. Furthermore, nearly all essential oils are toxic to cats and other pets. If you have pets, please consult your veterinarian before using any form of aromatherapy in your home.

HOW DOES AROMATHERAPY WORK?

Aromatherapy is a practice that dates back centuries. It involves using essential oils through smell, touch, or taste for therapeutic purposes. Essential oils are plant extracts that can be made with different parts of the plant by capturing the essence that creates fragrance. (Johns Hopkins Medicine, n.d.b).

Inhalation: When you breathe in the fragrance, the scent molecules travel to the amygdala in the brain, the center responsible for emotions.

Touch: Drops of essential oils can be added to oil for massage or to bathwater for a fragrant soak. They are often added to commercial skin and hair care products.

HOW TO USE ESSENTIAL OILS

Accessories: These are pieces of jewelry infused with essential oil that you can wear day or night to smell as needed.

Body Oil: Mixing concentrated essential oils that can irritate with a carrier oil dilutes them, lowering the risk of irritation.

Aroma Sticks or Inhalers: These are small capped sticks you uncap and bring to the nose to inhale when needed. They are portable and easy to use and store.

Diffusers: Diffusers can send the aroma of an oil to fill an entire room, so it is important to be sure that anyone who might be able to smell it, such as children, will be safe. It is best when used in a closed room or if you live alone (Johns Hopkins Medicine, n.d.b).

WHICH ESSENTIAL OILS ARE USED TO TREAT INSOMNIA?

1. **Lavender Oil:** Lavender oil is the most well-known and popular essential oil used for sleep difficulties. Numerous studies have cited its effectiveness. Other benefits of lavender oil include lowering heart rate, temperature, and blood pressure. Lavender oil is also known to reduce anxiety.

2. **Marjoram Oil:** Marjoram oil is popular because it doesn't just help with falling asleep; it is known to help keep you asleep. It has a sweet smell, known to produce the kind of deep, peaceful sleep where you truly heal and recharge.

3. **Sandalwood Oil:** Sandalwood oil is one of the most expensive oils on the list, but few oils are as effective at inducing deep rest. While other oils may slow heart rates or chase away troubling thoughts, sandalwood oil has mood-balancing properties that help you relax and unwind. The smell is rich and distinctive. If you find it too strong on its own, it can be used in a nighttime blend in small quantities.

4. **Bergamot Oil:** Bergamot oil is popular for its anti-inflammatory and anti-bacterial properties. It also reduces blood pressure and

heart rate and helps prepare the body for sleep. Additionally, bergamot oil has been shown to reduce stressful thoughts, often responsible for keeping us up at night.

5. **Ylang Ylang Oil:** Besides having a great name, ylang ylang oil is an excellent essential oil to use when sleep eludes you. The oil is an extract of a yellow flower from a tropical tree in Asia native to the Philippines and can lower blood pressure and heart rate. It also naturally sets the body up for sleep. The scent is somewhat fruity and calming and is a common addition to many skincare products as it can be applied to the skin. However, allergic reactions to topical application are not uncommon. Dog and cat lovers may want to be extra careful with this oil because while it is typically safe for people, it is toxic to cats and dogs via touch and ingestion (Intrepid Mental Wellness LLC, n.d.).

Acupuncture

You may be familiar with acupuncture to treat pain, but did you know that it can be used to treat a wide variety of concerns, such as allergies, depression, and - yes, even insomnia? Acupuncture is derived from ancient Chinese medicinal practices in which needles are inserted into the skin to treat various conditions. Traditionally, it is believed a life force, or Qi, runs through the body. The body can suffer illness when that life force is blocked or does not run freely. Acupuncture is believed to restore Qi to a natural state of flow.

Modern acupuncture is based on the belief that the needles stimulate sensory nerves under the skin that release natural substances, such as endorphins, to make you feel better (NHS, 2023). Whether looking at it from a traditional or a modern perspective, acupuncture is not a one-and-done treatment. A course of several sessions is typically recommended to reap the most benefits.

HOW IS ACUPUNCTURE PERFORMED?

The practitioner, or acupuncturist, will insert fine needles a few centimeters long into the skin at specific spots on the body, depending on what ails you. You will either be seated or lying down and may need to remove some clothing to provide access to the skin. Needles may be inserted very shallowly, just under the skin, or deeper to reach muscle, depending on what ails you.

The needles are left in place for anywhere from a few minutes to half an hour. Insertion of the needles may tingle, or you may feel an ache, but it should not hurt. If you experience a lot of pain, tell the practitioner immediately. Sometimes people experience side effects of the procedure, including pain or bruising, feeling dizzy or faint, or feeling sick (NHS, 2023).

ACUPUNCTURE FOR SLEEP

Acupuncture is used to treat different symptoms that can lead to poor sleep, including restless leg syndrome, depression and anxiety, pain, and sleep apnea. Any one of these can make a good night's sleep almost impossible. Acupuncture can often relieve these symptoms, removing significant barriers to falling and staying asleep all night.

Insomnia not caused by any specific cause is referred to as primary insomnia. There is less research on acupuncture's effectiveness in resolving this sleep problem. Still, some preliminary findings show that "traditional acupuncture was more effective at increasing sleep quality and daytime functioning than sham acupuncture or the sedative medication estazolam" (de Bellefonds, 2021). Acupuncture can be used in conjunction with other treatments or tried alone.

Acupressure

Acupressure is similar to acupuncture. However, it is non-invasive and involves gentle pressure instead of needles. The pressure is applied to specific points with your finger, thumb, knuckle, or a blunt object. It can release endorphins, clear up digestive issues, and promote sleep quality. Preliminary evidence suggests acupressure can help people with insomnia get better sleep.

I recommend having a session with a qualified, experienced practitioner before trying acupressure yourself. They will teach you the proper techniques and locations of the various pressure points. Do not use acupressure while pregnant without talking to your doctor first. If you feel pain or discomfort, just stop; It should feel good. Likewise, if you have injuries, numbness, or recent blood clots, don't use the pressure points in those areas. Widely considered safe, acupressure does not typically cause side effects. However, you might not experience the potential benefits if you do it incorrectly.

The recommended pressure points for sleep are:

- ☐ The middle of the foot, just behind the middle toe
- ☐ The inside of the lower leg, about four inches above the ankle
- ☐ The middle of the arm, about three inches from the hand
- ☐ The outside of the wrist
- ☐ About an inch behind the ear lobe
- ☐ Between the eyebrows.

Apply 30 seconds of pressure to each point on both sides of your body. You can do this on your own, or you may prefer to have a partner assist you. Though more research is needed, evidence shows acupressure can safely help people fall asleep (HealthMatch, 2022).

I suggest you use your favorite search engine on the web to find more detailed instructions, images, and videos should you decide to self-administer acupressure. Always discuss alternative treatments with your primary healthcare provider for best practice.

Emotional Freedom Technique (EFT)

EFT involves finger tapping on specified meridian acupressure points on the face, body, and hands; the specific points are the top of the head, the center of the forehead, the eyebrow, the side of the eye, under the eye, under the nose, the chin, collarbone, under arm and side of the hand. Dozens of randomized controlled trials suggest that EFT helps numerous conditions related to ADHD. Tapping helps relax the sympathetic nervous system, thus inducing a calmer, more relaxed state. It can be done with a practitioner or by oneself if learned properly. (ADDitude, 2021)

Here is the sequence for sleep:

1. Identify the problem and create a positive affirmation phrase - For example, I fully embrace my ADHD, and I will have a good night's sleep.

2. Using either your index finger or the fingertips of your right hand, tap your left hand's outer edge (karate chop area). Tap as you say your affirmation phrase three times. Repeat with the left fingertips tapping the side of the right hand.

3. Tap the other pressure points in the following sequence:

    ☐ Tap one eyebrow (close to the nose where the eyebrow starts).

    ☐ Tap the side of one eye (on the bone bordering the outside corner of the eye).

    ☐ Tap under one eye (on the bone about 1 inch below your pupil).

    ☐ Tap under the nose.

    ☐ Tap the chin (midway between your bottom lip and the bottom of your chin).

    ☐ Tap the collarbone (at the notch beneath the inside edge of the collarbone).

    ☐ Tap underarm (about 4 inches below the armpit).

    ☐ Tap the top center of the head.

4. Tap each point seven times. As you move on to a new point, recite your phrase to maintain focus on your affirmation.

5. Repeat the sequence two or three times, or until you are relaxed enough to fall asleep (Women's Health Network, 2023).

I recommend incorporating EFT into your nightly sleep hygiene routine. A consistent EFT practice with other evening unwinding activities will increase its effectiveness, as it is widely considered a complementary practice. Consider working with an EFT coach or therapist if you want additional support and guidance. They can teach you the proper technique and precise tapping points before you begin.

Remember, everyone's quest for better rest is unique. Experiment with different strategies and adapt them to your needs to find your best sleep solutions.

Mindfulness Meditation

Meditation as a practice has a long history in the East but has been gaining popularity around the world as a way to improve wellness in people of all ages, from children right up to seniors. Mindfulness meditation is the practice of meditating to bring your thoughts back to a place where you are observing how you are feeling and thinking without judgment. It is a way of letting go of the types of worries and anxieties that can paralyze the mind or send it in spirals of worry.

While you can use mindfulness meditation techniques any time, when used at night, the purpose is to relax the body and quiet the mind, preparing yourself for sleep. In many cases, the practice should result in falling asleep before the session ends. This is one of the most encouraged techniques to try when facing insomnia for several reasons.

1. **It's free.** No discrimination based on the ability to pay with this method. Yes, you can download paid apps or join a class to learn how to meditate, but neither is necessary to start a successful nightly meditation practice.

2. **It doesn't require any equipment.** Some people like to meditate on cushions or a chair, but lying in a comfortable position on your bed is perfectly fine, even encouraged with nighttime meditation.

3. **You don't have to go anywhere.** No driving, taking public transport, or stressing about making it to class on time. It is a solitary activity leading to sleep, so practicing in the comfort of your home (bed, specifically) is the way to go.

4. **It's easy.** Hear me out. When I say easy, I mean that the technique itself is simple. Just breathe in a calming rhythm while you bring your focus inward, relaxing your body and mind. Everyone knows that calming the mind in practice is much more difficult. However, the basic meditation techniques are not difficult to learn.

If you have struggled with meditating in the past, consider searching for guided sleep meditations online first. You can find several on

YouTube for free, and many free and paid applications are available. A guided meditation will walk you through the steps to take, and you can listen to them as many times as you want before you feel comfortable enough to try without the guiding voice.

Some Meditation Apps to Try

- ☐ Insight Timer
- ☐ Headspace
- ☐ Aura
- ☐ Calm
- ☐ Buddhify
- ☐ Ten Percent Happier

Research shows that meditation reduces pain sensitivity and enhances control over the autonomic nervous system. This, in turn, reduces the likelihood of waking up in the middle of the night. The benefits of sleep meditation extend to potentially alleviating conditions like depression and insomnia. Additionally, it can assist in resetting circadian rhythms. It is a safe and accessible alternative to pharmacological treatments for sleep disorders, and meditation can be used in conjunction with other therapies (Sleep Cycle, 2021).

Similar to acupuncture, the benefits take time to reach their peak. Ideally, you should make time to meditate nightly, but any consistent schedule is better than nothing.

In Chapter 8, we switch gears a little to step away from how to help adults sleep better and turn our attention to helping improve sleep in children.

CHAPTER 8

Sleep Tips for Parents of Children with ADHD

Alex, age 10, has been running up and down the hallway outside his bedroom for the past 20 minutes. Bedtime was at 8:30 p.m., but despite his parents' best efforts, he's nowhere near actually going to bed, and it's already 10:45 p.m. It's not that he's not tired. In fact, Alex is overtired and is experiencing a level of hyperactivity that has left his parents exhausted. They are waiting for him to completely wear himself out, which usually involves dissolving into a puddle of tears at some point before being able to put him down. They hope it will be for an entire night of sleep.

Alex's parents have tried everything they know. They give Alex lots of exercise in the afternoons and restrict sugary foods and drinks in the evenings. He has a set bedtime and a great bedtime routine that involves no screen time and a quiet activity with mom and dad before bed. Alex *goes* to bed without a fight. The problem is that he doesn't *stay* in bed. Within 10 minutes of saying goodnight, he's up again, telling his parents he isn't tired. They're at their wits' end and need some advice to help Alex fall asleep the first time he is put in bed.

Dealing with your own sleep issues is tricky, but add your kid's sleep issues to the mix, and that's when life can get really complicated. Children's sleep habits tend to be different from that of adults to begin with, so extra care is needed to be sure that the approaches we use to fix their sleep problems don't do more harm than good. Add ADHD to the mix, and there's a lot to consider.

The good news is that you're taking action early. By tackling sleep dysfunction early, you can help your child lay the foundations for healthy sleep habits that will serve them well for the rest of their lives. Some extra effort now can help the whole family get better sleep and set up your child's sleep habits for life.

Get Your Child Tested

Just like adults, children with ADHD can also have co-morbid conditions that make sleep more difficult. First, before you begin treating sleep dysfunction, you want to ensure you've ruled out everything else that may need to be addressed. We don't want to put our kids through unnecessary treatments or therapies if a simpler solution is available.

START WITH A SLEEP DIARY

A sleep diary is a snapshot of your child's sleep-wake schedule. On average, sleep diaries are kept for one to two weeks. If your child is old enough, they can keep it themselves with some supervision; otherwise, you can fill it out for them. It should include several pieces of information:

- ☐ Sleep and wake times
- ☐ Any nighttime wake-ups
- ☐ Dreams or nightmares
- ☐ Daytime sleepiness
- ☐ Food and drink consumed in the evening
- ☐ Exercise or other physical activity

□ Use of screens, hobbies, or other non-physical activity before bed.

A doctor or sleep specialist will use the information in the journal to pinpoint any patterns or potential areas of concern and determine the next steps (NYU Langone, n.d.).

SLEEPINESS SCALE

This is a questionnaire measuring your child's likeliness of feeling tired or dozing off during a variety of daytime scenarios. It is then assessed by a doctor or sleep specialist. These two items, the journal and the sleepiness scale results, are combined to decide if a sleep study is warranted.

SLEEP STUDY

A sleep study, or polysomnogram, is an overnight test that measures various functions in the body while your child sleeps. They are typically used to diagnose or rule out four conditions:

1. **Sleep apnea:** This can be a serious condition when breathing starts and stops throughout the night, which can be caused by multiple factors.

2. **Narcolepsy:** This is a neurological condition that hampers the brain's ability to control the sleep-wake cycle, resulting in a person feeling rested in the mornings but then progressively more tired as the day wears on. Narcolepsy can cause sudden bouts of sleepiness with little warning.

3. **Hypersomnia:** Hypersomnia is similar to narcolepsy in that individuals experience excessive daytime drowsiness, but there are some key differences. Those with hypersomnia sleep excessively, often having difficulty waking up in the morning,

feeling sleepy all day, and falling asleep during waking hours. They must experience daytime sleepiness every day for more than three months to receive a diagnosis.

4. **Periodic Limb Movement Disorder:** This disorder affects between 4% and 11% of the population. It is characterized by jerking, twitching, or cramping of the lower limbs specifically during sleep. It impacts sleep quality, even when an individual does not wake up completely from it. It causes daytime fatigue as a result (Foley, 2023).

A sleep study is typically done in a sleep clinic with a specialized doctor. The process can be a bit overwhelming, especially for young children, so talking about what will happen in advance is crucial. A technician will place sensors in several spots on the child, including the head, eyes, chin, and legs. They will also put a belt around their stomach area to measure breathing. None of these things should hurt, but they can be a bit strange and uncomfortable for sleeping. A microphone and camera will also record the session. A parent is allowed to stay during the session.

The study checks for things like eye movement, heart rate, breathing, brain waves, blood oxygen level, carbon dioxide levels, snoring, body movements, sleep positions, and sleep stages (Nemours Kids Health, n.d.). Results may take a few weeks to become available.

BLOOD TEST

If your child has difficulty falling asleep or moves a lot before sleep, they may be suffering from restless leg syndrome, which we discussed in an earlier chapter. Low iron levels can worsen the symptoms of restless leg syndrome, so a blood test may be ordered to rule it out.

Sleep Hygiene

Sleep hygiene for children is extremely important. As a parent, you are essentially teaching your child the habits they will take with them into adulthood. It isn't always easy to implement these habits with kids. First, consistency is important, and life with children is often unpredictable. Life with a child with ADHD is even more unpredictable. Second, children grow and change so quickly that something like a set bedtime will need to change over time as well. Finally, many of us haven't thought much about our own sleep habits and just assume that kids will sleep when they're tired as long as they are safe and comfortable. That may be true for some children, but as you know, ADHD is a different story.

You will recognize some of the recommended sleep hygiene habits for children from the chapter on sleep hygiene for adults, but there are some key differences.

BEDTIME ROUTINE

Let's start with the most obvious. Did your child have a bedtime routine when they were toddlers that they have since grown out of but not replaced with anything effective? Or do you have a teenager who isn't interested in a story and a cuddle before sleep? Everyone needs a bedtime routine, from babies to adults, so let's talk about the basics. Let's be honest. Kids with ADHD who already have sleep dysfunction are likely not to want to go to sleep, so we need to make the entire process as painless as possible.

1. **After dinner:** Once children are finished eating dinner, there is typically an hour or more before bedtime. At this time, electronics and stimulating activities should be replaced with quiet, non-digital alternatives. Board games, drawing or other

artistic activities, and building with blocks are all ways to avoid the blue light from screens that can make our brains more alert. Children with ADHD need longer to wind down to a place where sleep is possible than children without ADHD, so you have to start early to be ready in time for bed (Next Step 4 ADHD, 2020).

2. **Bedtime:** Set a bedtime that is the same all week, even on weekends, with young children, and try to encourage that as much as possible with teenagers. Wake-up time should also remain steady. That may mean some earlier weekend mornings than you or your teen would like, but it will help keep their circadian rhythm on track.

3. **Bath, shower, or other form of relaxation for the body:** Warm water helps make children drowsy, so a quiet bath or shower can be a good idea. If baths mean playtime, perhaps a warm shower will do the trick. Finish with brushing teeth and other grooming activities, then put on pajamas.

4. **Relaxation:** Children can learn yoga, mindfulness breathing, meditation, or any number of relaxation techniques to help quiet the body and mind. This can signal that the day is done, it's time to relax, and it's time to sleep. Older children may even prefer to journal or use a guided meditation app.

5. **Book or other quiet wrap-up activity before sleep:** Younger children may enjoy being read to in bed (older ones, too.). Teens might want to read alone, draw, journal, or listen to some relaxing music before sleep. Try to choose the same activity each night to create an association of the activity with sleep.

SLEEP ENVIRONMENT

1. **Bedroom:** Create a calming sleep environment. Kids' rooms often double as a play space or hangout spot. If the walls or bedding are bright, the lighting is harsh, and toys, screens, or other distractions are everywhere, it's time to rethink things. Calm colors, some soft lamps for the evening, and a cabinet that can hide away toys or the television in a teen's room can remove some of the visual clutter and create a relaxed environment. While trying to establish better sleep habits, consider cutting off play or hanging-out time in the bedroom for an hour before sleep to break the association with daytime activities.

2. **Noise:** The ADHD brain sometimes likes to latch on to noises that do nothing but distract them. If you live close to a busy street or are in a house or apartment where the bedrooms are close to the living spaces, the noise might be enough to keep your child from falling asleep. Consider some form of white noise, such as a fan or white noise machine, to drown out those sounds. For some children, nature sounds such as running water work better, so try a few different ones until you find something that works.

3. **Light:** Light signals to the brain that it is time to wake up and be alert for the day ahead, so limiting light in a child's room is essential. Blackout curtains can help keep out lights from streetlights or any other outdoor light that may enter through windows. If your child is afraid of the dark, consider a small night light in the hallway rather than the bedroom itself or a motion-sensor night light that will turn on if the child gets out of bed. Teens may consider keeping their bedroom door closed or using a sleep mask.

4. **Interruptions:** It can be hard to stop all interruptions, especially if you have more than one child, including an infant who may cry

and wake everyone up, or two children who share a bedroom but
not the same bedtime. Closing their bedroom door, using white
noise machines, and keeping pets from the bedroom can help
minimize the distractions you can control.

5. **Weighted Blanket:** Weighted blankets should be purchased to
    weigh only between 5% and 10% of the child's body weight for
    safety reasons. They work by helping put light pressure on the
    body, providing the person using it with a feeling of safety and
    security and promoting relaxation. For those who like them, a
    weighted blanket can feel like a warm hug. They are also less
    likely to fall off a child during the night; this prevents a child
    from waking up due to cold.

Lifestyle Considerations

It's a bit odd to think of "lifestyle considerations" when talking
about children. Still, it's just about ensuring they are set up for the
best possible night's sleep they can get regularly. Being overly rigid or
strict doesn't work with most kids, and with ADHDers, flexibility is
crucial. Making an effort to follow the suggestions as often as
possible without taking them overboard is key.

Food

Most kids love food and aren't particularly concerned about whether
that second slice of cake will keep them up until midnight. As adults,
we know which foods we eat, in what quantities, and when can affect
more than just our taste buds. A child's diet should include
everything in moderation, but when it comes to sleep, there are
certain foods and drinks that work against it.

1. **Sugar:** Almost everyone likes sugar, but sugary treats in the evenings will likely keep your child from getting a good night's sleep. If possible, save foods with added sugar for earlier in the day or serve it with a meal to slow the absorption. Remember, natural sugars count, so natural fruit juice isn't any better than cookies when it comes to sleep.

2. **Caffeine:** Your five-year-old probably isn't sipping on an espresso, but your teen might enjoy a cup of coffee or an energy drink full of caffeine. Caffeine is a stimulant, and while we know that stimulants tend to have a calming effect on people with ADHD, much like stimulant medication, it is typically not recommended too late in the day as it can interfere with sleep. Talk to your teen about limiting caffeinated beverages to the first half of the day and switching to non-caffeinated drinks in the afternoon.

3. **Dinner:** Schedule dinner at least a few hours before bedtime to allow for digestion. Avoid heavy or greasy foods and large portions too close to bed. They may leave kids feeling heavy, bloated, or uncomfortable. It may also increase the need to move, making settling difficult. A light meal in the evenings is best. If your child has a snack in the evenings, consider something higher in protein and lower in carbohydrates or sugars.

Exercise

Exercise is a great way to manage some ADHD attributes and help your child get a good night's sleep. Exercising earlier in the day is preferable because the subsequent energy spike isn't helpful right before bed. Current recommendations are for children to get an hour of aerobic activity daily, so this is a great way to meet that general health recommendation while supporting another healthy habit:

sleep. A gentle yoga or stretching routine at night can help relax your child, while more vigorous exercise should be saved for the morning or early afternoon hours.

Falling and Staying Asleep

As many parents know, even with everything in place, it can still not be enough to get your child to fall asleep. Even after drifting off, it's not uncommon to have them wake up in the middle of the night. Following the above suggestions is a good start, particularly the white noise and dark room, because it can help lull a child back to sleep if they wake up before morning. Still, there are some other treatments to consider.

Giving children supplements or medication, even over-the-counter meds, can be risky without the guidance of a doctor, so always check with a medical professional first.

1. **Melatonin:** This hormone is a popular over-the-counter supplement available in most drug and grocery stores in the U.S. It is marketed for children as young as 3 years old to help them fall asleep.

2. **Over-the-counter Antihistamines:** As discussed in previous chapters, these tend to work for a short period only as the body gradually adapts, thus requiring higher doses over time. Children should never exceed recommended doses.

3. **Prescription Medication:** There are no FDA-approved insomnia drugs for children. Doctors may prescribe a medication that has sedative effects meant to treat another condition in what is known as "off-label" prescriptions, with the hope that it will address the sleep issues in a child.

4. **Aromatherapy:** Aromatherapy can be used with children, though proceed with caution and make sure you choose the appropriate essential oils, formulations, and delivery methods suitable for children. Be aware of the toxicity to pets.

5. **Sleep Tea:** Some nighttime or sleep teas are safe for children and can be used with aromatherapy or other quiet rituals. Talk to your doctor before administering any herbal teas to minors.

After talking to their doctor, Alex's parents have made some additional changes to his nighttime routine. Alex now takes melatonin to help him fall asleep at a more appropriate time for his age. They take him outside for some exercise after dinner to help with digestion and to get some extra energy out. Alex also now does some mindfulness breathing and guided meditation for kids with his parents each night, and his parents have added blackout curtains to his room and a white noise machine to drown out the sounds of the household. His doctor approved certain aromatherapy and nighttime teas as well.

Altogether, the added changes are working; Alex is now routinely asleep by 9:30 p.m. It's not quite the bedtime his parents want, but it's a significant improvement, and they hope that with consistency, things will continue to get better.

CHAPTER 9

New Parents, Teens, and Young Adults

"The very traits that once held Ty back are now his greatest assets."

—Yvonne Pennington, mother of
Ty Pennington (ADDitude, 2020).

Chapter 8 covered helping young children get better sleep, but infants and teens are separate categories that deserve their own special sections.

New Parents

Sleepless nights are pretty much the norm for many parents from the newborn to toddler years, but when you're already dealing with ADHD-related sleep concerns, it can become overwhelming. Getting enough sleep when you have a new baby, especially one who is nursing, can be challenging. While some new mothers choose not to take any medications at all while breastfeeding, many ADHD drugs are considered safe to keep taking. Before breastfeeding, make sure you discuss any medications you may be taking with your doctor and get approval to continue (Ramirez et al., n.d.).

Parents of babies need to prioritize self-care, even though that may seem impossible. Breastfeeding mothers may consider pumping and having a partner take overnight feedings on a rotational basis to allow for better sleep. Bottle-feeding parents can start this process from an early age more easily. The old advice to "sleep when the baby sleeps" is often difficult to follow. Taking time to nap for 20 minutes a few times during the day isn't exactly the recommended 7 or more hours of sleep, but it can help in the short term to increase the total amount of sleep in a 24-hour period.

Post-partum depression can negatively affect sleep in women. Many new fathers also experience difficulty sleeping as well as depression or enhanced anxiety as they adjust to their new life. Don't hesitate to reach out to support groups or your doctor to talk about any new feelings that may indicate a mental health concern so it can be treated promptly, which may improve sleep and coping abilities. Also, to the extent possible, create a conducive sleep environment and continue to practice sleep hygiene. If your baby is sleeping in your room, things like keeping the room dark and quiet will help your baby sleep longer and more soundly.

It can be difficult to manage the effects of sleeplessness that come with the first year of a new baby, as well as the regular ADHD symptoms you may routinely experience. During this period, you may need to speak with your doctor to see if there are changes to medication or treatments that could be temporarily beneficial or if there are additional therapies that could help you through what is a wonderful time for your family but a trying time for sleep!

The Teen Years

If you have a teenager, you know that the suggestions in Chapter 8 may sound great, but convincing your teen to follow them is more complex than getting your eight-year-old on board. Adolescence is a complicated period, both biologically and socially. Your teen wants more independence and control over their decisions but also needs guidance to help them through the big changes they are experiencing in their bodies and minds.

Adolescence is a transitional period from the early teenage years to the late teens or early twenties, including physical, emotional, and cognitive changes. On a physical level, adolescence is marked by the onset of puberty, which usually begins to happen around age 11 or 12. In addition to the physical changes, it is a time of intense emotional and mental changes. Teens develop a sense of independence but are not yet adults. They face different types of peer pressure and self-identity exploration while they start to experiment with more adult behavior. Teens want to go out more with friends on the weekends and may start desiring a later bedtime on Friday and Saturday nights than the rest of the week to accommodate their changing social life.

From a sleep perspective, adolescence is when the body's circadian clock changes. Rather than feeling tired between 8:00 p.m. and 9:00 p.m., the onset of those feelings of tiredness shifts back by about two hours, kicking in usually between 10:00 pm and 11:00 p.m. This is officially called a *sleep phase delay*. You may notice sometime around the age of 11 or 12 that your child begins having more difficulty falling asleep at their regular bedtime. This is normal.

Unfortunately, this shift in sleep onset also comes with an accompanying shift in wake-up times, meaning that your child who was always up and ready for school by 7:30 am, now probably isn't ready to get up much before 9 am. Getting your teen up on time for school is a common parent complaint. Your teen may want to go to sleep two hours later, but they still need to wake up at the same time, which can cause a loss of two hours of sleep a night on average. This is particularly dangerous for their health and development, as teens need, on average, nine hours of sleep a night. As more research comes out on this phenomenon, some high schools are actually transitioning to later start times to better accommodate the natural sleep patterns of teens (UCLA Health, n.d.).

Parents are significant factors in helping teens navigate these changes. The goal is to help young teens set up good sleep habits and then eventually hand over responsibility for maintaining those habits to them as they get closer to adulthood. This book can be an excellent resource to help them do that.

Teens who have never exhibited ADHD symptoms before are often mistaken for having ADHD if they have poor sleep patterns. We already know how lack of sleep can mimic the signs of ADHD and how it can make the symptoms of ADHD exponentially worse for someone already diagnosed.

Most teens and parents know that they aren't getting enough sleep, but few people understand the true extent of the problem. Research shows that only 8% of American teenagers get the recommended 9 hours of sleep at night, and a full 59% live with chronic sleep deprivation, meaning they sleep less than 6 hours a night on average (Garey, 2023). The long-term consequences can be severe.

HELPING YOUR TEEN GET MORE SLEEP

- ☐ **Be aware of their load:** School, home life, chores, sports, and social commitments can make teens even busier than adults. Help reduce the load where possible.

- ☐ **Keep them on a regular sleep/wake schedule.** This can be tough on weekends, as adolescents start going out later at night or wanting to stay up playing video games. Allowing your child to stay up until 2:00 am Friday nights and sleep until noon on Saturdays is risking making sleep difficulties worse.

- [ ] **If your child is exhausted on weekends, they can safely sleep in for up to two hours past their regular wake-up time.** After that, it can cause even more problems with the circadian clock.

- [ ] **Encourage your teen to avoid nicotine, alcohol, and other drugs.** They are terrible for the body and interfere with sleep.

- [ ] **Limit evening screen time and have a rule about electronics in the bedroom overnight.** This is particularly important if you go to bed before your teen. Having cell phones and video game consoles in their bedroom can be too tempting for the average teen, especially if you are already asleep and unable to make sure they aren't using them when they should be sleeping.

- [ ] **No caffeine (including coffee, caffeinated teas, energy drinks, or chocolate) past 4:00 p.m.** (UCLA Health, n.d.).

- [ ] **If your child has a part-time job, it should end in the evenings by 9:00 p.m.** to allow enough time to get home and ready for bed by 11:00 p.m. at the latest.

- [ ] **Model good sleep hygiene yourself.**

- [ ] **Limit nighttime snacking.**

- [ ] **Streamline mornings so your teen can sleep as much as possible on weekdays.** An extra 30 minutes daily can give your child another 2.5 hours of sleep a week.

- [ ] **Help your child take control of their sleep.** Consider using sleep apps that allow them to track their sleep and support them in their efforts to make helpful changes.

College, Roommates, and Other Cohabitation Situations

Many sleep hygiene suggestions assume that you have a certain amount of control over your sleeping arrangements, like the ability to dim your lights in the evening, create a calm and quiet environment, or use aromatherapy oils without annoying anyone else in the process. This isn't always the case, and for many young adults, moving out of their parents' home after high school to go away for college or share an apartment with roommates is the first time they are responsible for their own sleep habits, and must do so in an environment over which they only have partial control.

College dorms, fraternity or sorority houses, or even off-campus housing aren't generally known for their lights out at 10:00 p.m. policy. Sharing a dorm room with another person or an apartment with 4 roommates who are more interested in partying than resetting their circadian clock can make it difficult to maintain good sleep habits. Most college students or young adults living independently for the first time can get swept up in the freedom of living entirely by their own rules until sleep problems interfere with their quality of life.

Young adult ADHDers may find that this happens sooner rather than later and need to figure out how to make it work in a space that often provides little privacy and a less-than-conducive environment for getting seven or more hours of sleep a night.

SOME TIPS FOR BETTER SLEEP

- ☐ **Be realistic.** Unless you live alone, there will likely be times when your sleep schedule will be interrupted. Being overly rigid can lead to more problems than solutions.

- [ ] **Agree on certain boundaries.** Perhaps Friday and Saturday nights are anything goes with your roommates, but weeknights are quiet after midnight.

- [ ] **Use the tools available.** A weighted blanket, a sleep mask, noise-canceling headphones or white noise app, aromatherapy pillow spray and sleep teas are all tools you can use to help improve your sleep without insisting that everyone around you go to sleep at the same time.

- [ ] **Try to schedule classes later in the morning** if you know it will be challenging to go to sleep early.

- [ ] **Practice stress reduction strategies** and set a cut-off time for things like homework, caffeine, or alcohol consumption to make falling asleep easier.

- [ ] **Get enough exercise** to try and tire yourself out physically during the day so you can sleep at night.

- [ ] **Practice getting outside first thing in the morning** to help reset your circadian rhythm.

Not all people who share living spaces are college students or young adults, but many of these suggestions apply to any age. Control what is within your control, compromise with your roommates to keep the peace for everyone, and work with what you have available.

CHAPTER 10

Advice for Irregular Circumstances

This chapter covers a few irregular circumstances not addressed previously. Maybe you are the partner of someone with ADHD who is experiencing difficulties, or you work shifts and you can't apply many of the sleep hygiene recommendations, or you have really young kids. The combination of multiple wake-ups and your own sleep troubles is making it impossible for you to function on a daily basis. This chapter is for you.

Not everyone can dedicate the time to create a pre-sleep routine that involves a gentle winding down from the day, a consistent bedtime, and eight hours of uninterrupted sleep. That doesn't mean you can't make some changes to improve your chances of getting the best night's sleep possible under the circumstances.

Shift Work, Sleep Disorders, and ADHD

Shift work, in general, is associated with increased sleep problems. When you add ADHD to the mix, the effects can be even more severe. Shift work sleep disorder (SWSD) is a circadian rhythm sleep disorder that affects people who work overnight, early morning, or rotating shifts. Having inconsistent sleep/wake times can mess with your circadian rhythm and internal clock, which we discussed in more detail in earlier chapters. Shift work is unnatural to the biological clock and results mainly in problems falling asleep, staying asleep, or with unwanted sleepiness. It is prevalent, affecting between 10% and 40% of shift workers in the United States, and can be diagnosed if symptoms are experienced for more than three months (Cleveland Clinic, 2021b).

Knowing what we do about ADHD's impact on sleep problems, it's no surprise that people with ADHD who work shifts may be at an even heightened risk of severe symptoms from SWSD.

If changing your schedule isn't possible—and let's be honest, we can't all quit our jobs to better suit our sleep schedule—consider implementing some strategies to help trick your circadian rhythm into cooperating.

- [ ] If you need to sleep during the day, wear dark sunglasses on your way home after a night shift.
- [ ] Try napping before a night shift.
- [ ] Avoid frequently rotating shifts; try to work the same shift for as long as possible.
- [ ] Consume caffeine at the beginning of a shift, but not at the end so it doesn't interfere with sleep.
- [ ] Try to keep a regular sleep schedule at home that allows for a minimum of 7 hours of sleep.
- [ ] Practice good sleep hygiene within the constraints of your schedule.
- [ ] If you must sleep during the day while others are at home or there is a lot of ambient noise, consider noise-canceling headphones and an eye mask or blackout curtains.
- [ ] Try interventions such as bright light therapy in the form of a light box, desk lamp, or goggles at the beginning of your shift and melatonin or medications after it (Cleveland Clinic, 2021b).

Air Travel

Traveling for business or vacation can wreak havoc on your sleep. Airplane travel, different time zones, irregular sleeping patterns, dietary changes, and more can throw off anyone's system. As we know, while most people can return to a regular sleep schedule soon after returning from travel, it takes longer for the ADHD brain to return to normal.

There are, however, things you can do to minimize these adverse effects on sleep before, during, and after travel.

BEFORE TRAVEL

- ☐ Keep a sleep schedule as steady as possible before you leave for your trip.
- ☐ Purchase any sleep aids you may need in advance.

DURING TRAVEL

- ☐ Consider a sleep kit for the plane: noise-canceling headphones, a sleep mask, comfortable clothing, and a travel blanket.
- ☐ Limit caffeine and alcohol on the airplane.
- ☐ Try to adapt to a new time zone as soon as possible. Stay up until a reasonable bedtime and consider using melatonin to get to sleep.
- ☐ Bring some sleep essentials to the hotel room, including an aromatherapy candle, sleepy teas, or even your own pillow.
- ☐ Avoid too many late nights, heavy meals close to bedtime, or excess caffeine or alcohol.
- ☐ If noise is a problem, consider noise-canceling headphones or a white noise app.
- ☐ Consider guided sleep meditation apps to help you fall asleep.

- ☐ Try to readjust to the new time zone as quickly as possible.
- ☐ Return to your regular sleep routine the first night home to get your body back on schedule.
- ☐ Be patient if it takes longer than you would like to readjust.

Supporting Your Partner

Perhaps you aren't the one with ADHD but are supporting your partner. Staying up late once in a while and reverting back to a regular sleep schedule may be no big deal for you, or insomnia may be something you've heard about but never actually experienced yourself. How can you support your partner's struggles without being overbearing or taking on responsibility for them?

Andrea is the only member of her family not to have ADHD. Her husband was late-diagnosed but exhibits many of the most common attributes, including constantly losing track of what he's supposed to be doing, forgetting to put things away or close cabinet doors, and often not thinking through decisions before acting on them. While Mike, her husband, can fall asleep without any issues, he has difficulty staying asleep and often falls asleep at work during the day.

To make matters more complicated, their two boys also have ADHD. Their youngest is much like Alex, the little boy from earlier, who manages to go to bed but rarely manages to fall asleep much before midnight, resulting in difficulties at school the next day. Their oldest is a teenager who often stays up too late playing video games and then struggles to get up for school. Mornings are a challenge, and Andrea has trouble knowing how to help everyone. She feels that if she can start by supporting her partner, they could turn to help their kids get better sleep together.

A four-step approach is a great way to start.

1. **Be patient:** Getting sleep right with ADHD isn't always easy, and it often takes a lot of trial and error before finding the right mix of sleep hygiene, lifestyle changes, and even medication to be successful. And just when they think they've figured it out, something will change, and they have to start all over again.

    Trust me, it's as painful for your partner as it is for you. Encourage their efforts and be patient with how long it can all take. Making them more anxious whenever an intervention doesn't work worsens the problem.

2. **Practice sleep hygiene with your partner:** Changing sleep habits can be challenging, and if your partner is putting their electronics away an hour before bed to do yoga and meditate while you are playing games on your phone into the wee hours of the morning, it can be hard for them to follow through. Making sleep hygiene practices a couples' activity can help them stick to it and see success more quickly.

3. **Help them stay on track:** It is not your responsibility to take over your partner's plan for improving sleep. However, if your partner has difficulty with things like executive functioning skills or making and sticking to a schedule, you may be able to help them in these areas. Perhaps inspiring them to download and use apps that support their plan, creating a schedule and reminding them to stick to it when they struggle, or leading by example can help your partner keep on track.

4. **Celebrate success:** Sleep problems won't disappear overnight, and it can be frustrating and demoralizing to work so hard and feel like you aren't seeing progress. Celebrating small successes, like

falling asleep 30 minutes earlier than usual or sleeping all through the night, is worth it and can keep momentum going.

It's not always easy to be the support partner, so if you need to take a break occasionally, let your partner know. Take care of yourself first so you can better support your partner.

Autism

Research shows that for those with autism, there is a 50%-70% prevalence of ADHD as a comorbid condition (Hours, 2022). Autism comes with sleep challenges all its own, so for families whose children present with both, additional strategies may be needed to help get sleep on track. If you are an adult with both ADHD and autism (a combination unofficially termed AuDHD), these strategies apply equally to children and adults.

Autistic individuals have higher rates of sleep disruption than the general population, including insomnia genetic mutations that affect melatonin production and the circadian rhythm. They also get less REM sleep than those without autism. Non-autistic people spend about 25% of their time in REM sleep, while autistic individuals only spend 15% on average (Neff, n.d.). When combined with ADHD, sleep concerns can be significant. They may also be more likely to suffer from gastrointestinal distress or sensory issues that make relaxation difficult.

Autistic individuals often have different triggers for sleep difficulties than ADHDers.

- ☐ **Environmental triggers:** Autistic people are often bothered by external stimuli, making it difficult to turn off the world around them. Sounds, smells, and textures can be so distracting or upsetting that the individual finds it difficult to focus on anything else and has trouble relaxing. Audiobooks, soft music, white noise machines, fans, or sleep apps with nature sounds can drown out distracting sounds. Aromatherapy can ensure that household smells don't distract from sleep. Weighted blankets, soft sheets, and comfortable pajamas can make bedtime comforting.

- [ ] **Situational triggers:** Change is difficult for most people but can be particularly disruptive for those with autism. Disruptions in routine, illness, work schedule, or other changes can be particularly upsetting to autistic individuals. Keep a sleep and wake schedule whenever possible, and return to a regular schedule as quickly as possible if it is disrupted. Preparing for change ahead of time can also be helpful. Daylight Savings Time, in particular, can wreak havoc on sleep habits. A close friend informed me it takes her at least a week before she feels somewhat adjusted each time the clock moves forward or back an hour, and for many others on the autism spectrum, it can take 2-3 weeks to fully adapt to time changes (Duffy, 2017).

- [ ] **Social triggers:** Autistic people tend to have heightened sensitivity to outside stimuli and to the behaviors and moods of others. Attending social events, dealing with housemates, and even the mood changes of intimate partners can all lead to distress or difficulty relaxing and falling asleep. Those with both autism and ADHD often have competing sensibilities. The ADHD brain often seeks novelty and excitement and can enjoy large crowds, while autism often requires a significant amount of recovery time following social interactions. A good strategy is to take enough time before bedtime to recover following a social event so it doesn't interrupt sleep.

- [ ] **Emotional triggers:** Strong emotions are a common cause of sleep disturbance for most people, but for autistic individuals, emotions such as anxiety, sadness, stress, or anger can be all-consuming and difficult to suppress enough to fall asleep. Practicing guided meditation or journaling can help manage any feelings that may have come up during the day so that they don't interfere with sleep at night (Neff, n.d.).

Many of the same approaches mentioned in the chapter on sleep hygiene are applicable here, with some modifications according to the needs of the individual. Unlike ADHD, autism can present in many forms, so the sensory and overall support needs may vary significantly from person to person.

You may find suggestions for other irregular circumstances not covered in the book by exploring the resource section following the conclusion.

Conclusion

Andrea, the mom from Chapter 10 who is the only one in her family not to have ADHD, confesses that it's not all difficult nights and barely controlled chaos.

The traits that initially drew her to her husband, including his sense of adventure, curiosity about the world around him, and general love of life, are now traits that she loves about her boys. They may not always go to sleep on time, but they have spent many nights cuddling under the covers, enjoying one last bedtime story, or watching the sunrise on a warm summer morning when one of her boys wakes up earlier than she ever would without them.

Her boys are always ready for adventure, and their genuine interest in the world around them always makes them fun to be around. Andrea isn't interested in taking away their ADHD, just in helping make the more difficult parts easier for them to manage.

Improving sleep for ADHDers like me is a crucial aspect of helping ensure that the awesome bits of ADHD are not overshadowed by chronic fatigue. In this book, we have explored the relationship between sleep and ADHD, the effects of sleep deprivation on ADHD symptoms, and the impact of ADHD on sleep. We have also discussed sleep hygiene tips, medications, cognitive-behavioral therapy (CBT), and complementary and alternative medicine (CAM) for people with ADHD.

ADHD is responsible for helping me think outside the box and approach life with a creative and curious mind. However, it is also a neurodevelopmental condition that affects attention, hyperactivity, and impulsivity. It can make it difficult for me and fellow ADHDers to fall asleep and stay asleep. Sleep deprivation can lead to emotional dysregulation and behavioral problems and impact executive function, attention, impulse control, cognitive function, mood, and behavior. And that makes it hard to let the best parts of ADHD shine through.

My purpose in writing this book was to give others experiencing similar sleep difficulties some tools to get them back on the right track to a better quality of life through improved sleep. Understanding how sleep affects ADHD and how ADHD, in turn, affects our ability to get a good night's sleep is essential to being able to tackle the issue directly. I hope this book has simplified the extensive, often contradictory information to distill it into an easy-to-understand core that forms the basis of your personalized sleep improvement plan.

I recommend starting with the basics, which aren't always top of the list for an ADHD mind that craves novelty, not routine. Establishing a regular sleep schedule, creating a relaxing bedtime routine, making sure your bedroom is conducive to sleep, avoiding caffeine and alcohol before bed, and getting regular exercise are some of the sleep hygiene tips that can help improve sleep quality and quantity. For me personally, turning off screens an hour or two before bed is my first point of action. I also find it helpful to spend a few minutes writing in a journal before bed to help clear my mind. I have created a companion book - *The Quest for Better Rest Sleep Solutions Journal.* It is designed to assist in monitoring sleep habits, creating bedtime routines, developing better sleep hygiene, figuring out your personal sleep solutions, and enabling you to journal—all in one book. You can find it on Amazon.com along with my other published works.

Sometimes, changing your environment isn't enough, and that's where medications can come into play. Considering whether to change your dose of ADHD medication, add an over-the-counter sleep aid, or opt for a more powerful prescription option should be done carefully and in consultation with your doctor. Each option comes with benefits and risks to consider before choosing the proper medication.

Other alternate and complementary therapies are also worth considering. Cognitive-behavioral therapy for insomnia (CBT-I) is a type of talk therapy that can help people with sleep problems by changing thoughts and behaviors that interfere with sleep. CBT techniques include stimulus control, sleep restriction, relaxation training, cognitive restructuring, and psychoeducation. Complementary and alternative medicine (CAM), such as acupuncture, yoga, aromatherapy, and supplements like valerian root and chamomile, can also be used to treat sleep problems in people with ADHD.

Of course, helping children with ADHD to avoid becoming adults with sleep dysfunction is a huge priority. Sleep problems can start early; by cultivating good sleep hygiene at a young age and addressing issues as they emerge, the next generation can grow into adults who know how to manage bouts of insomnia like pros.

If you want to learn more about the topics in this book, check out some of the following resources. Remember that best practices change regularly as scientists and doctors publish their research, so it's important to update your knowledge occasionally. While I hope the contents of this book help you achieve that best rest experience, please be aware it may take weeks or months to find your personal sleep solutions. With discoveries in sleep science on the horizon, even if none of my strategies work for you now, there is always hope for help in the future.

If you enjoyed this book, please leave a review on my Amazon
Author page *and consider sharing it with friends and family.*

Thank you!

Resources

1. **ADDitude:** ADDitude is a leading source of information, advice, and support for individuals with ADHD and their families. They offer articles, webinars, and a vibrant online community.

   Website: ADDitude

2. **ADHD Online:** Description: ADHD Online is an online platform providing resources, education, and support for people living with ADHD. They offer a variety of educational materials and online courses.

   Website: ADHD Online

3. **American Academy of Sleep Medicine (AASM):** AASM is a professional organization that focuses on sleep medicine and sleep disorders. They provide resources for both healthcare professionals and the public.

   Website: AASM

4. **American Sleep Apnea Association (ASAA):** ASAA is dedicated to reducing the impact of sleep apnea through education, advocacy, and research. They offer information, support, and community resources.

   Website: ASAA

5. **Center for ADHD:** The Center for ADHD at the University of Maryland offers clinical services, research, and educational resources related to ADHD.

   Website: Center for ADHD

6. **Children and Adults with Attention-Deficit/Hyperactivity Disorder (CHADD):** CHADD is a national nonprofit organization providing education, support, and advocacy for individuals with ADHD and their families.

   Website: <u>CHADD</u>

7. **National Center on Sleep Disorders Research (NCSDR):** The NCSDR is a division of the National Heart, Lung, and Blood Institute, focusing on sleep disorders research. They offer information and resources on sleep disorders.

   Website: <u>NCSDR</u>

8. **Narcolepsy Network:** Narcolepsy Network is a nonprofit organization dedicated to improving the lives of people with narcolepsy and other sleep disorders. They provide education and support.

   Website: <u>Narcolepsy Network</u>

9. **National Sleep Foundation (NSF):** The NSF is dedicated to improving sleep health and well-being. They offer educational resources and information on a wide range of sleep topics.

   Website: <u>National Sleep Foundation</u>

10. **Sleep Education:** Sleep Education, provided by the American Academy of Sleep Medicine, offers comprehensive information and resources on various sleep disorders and healthy sleep habits.

    Website: <u>Sleep Education</u>

11. **Sleep Research Society (SRS):** SRS is a professional organization dedicated to advancing sleep and circadian research. They provide resources and support for researchers and clinicians.

    Website: <u>SRS</u>

12. **Sleeping Disorders Institute (SDI):** SDI offers diagnostic services, treatments, and resources for various sleep disorders. They have sleep clinics and educational materials.

    Website: <u>Sleeping Disorders Institute</u>

13. **The Attention Deficit Disorder Association (ADDA):** ADDA is a nonprofit organization that provides support, resources, and community for adults with ADHD. They focus on personal and professional development.

    Website: <u>ADDA</u>

14. **The Sleep Association:** The Sleep Association is an online resource center providing information on sleep disorders, treatments, and sleep-related topics for the public.

    Website: <u>The Sleep Association</u>

15. **The Sleep Health Foundation:** The Sleep Health Foundation, based in Australia, offers information and resources on sleep health and sleep disorders for the general public and healthcare professionals.

    Website: <u>The Sleep Health Foundation</u>

16. **The Sleep Research Society (SRS):** SRS is a professional organization that promotes the advancement of sleep research and education. They offer resources and support for researchers and clinicians.

    Website: <u>The Sleep Research Society (SRS)</u>

17. **The Sleep School:** The Sleep School provides online sleep education and resources to help individuals improve their sleep and overcome insomnia and sleep disorders.

    Website: <u>The Sleep School</u>

18. **The Sleep Wellness Institute:** The Sleep Wellness Institute is a comprehensive sleep center offering diagnostic services, treatments, and education on various sleep disorders.

    Website: <u>The Sleep Wellness Institute</u>

19. **Wake Up Narcolepsy:** Wake Up Narcolepsy is a nonprofit organization dedicated to raising awareness and providing support for people with narcolepsy and other sleep disorders.

    Website: <u>Wake Up Narcolepsy</u>

20. **World Sleep Society:** World Sleep Society is an international organization dedicated to advancing sleep medicine and sleep research. They provide resources and information on sleep health.

    Website: <u>World Sleep Society</u>

Please note that the availability of services and resources may vary by organization and location, so visiting their websites for more information is advisable. The websites mentioned above were correct as of the date of publication. However, they may change occasionally, so I suggest doing a web search for the desired organization if the link doesn't work.

References

ADDitude Editors. (2020, January 14). *10 ADHD quotes to save for a bad day*. ADDitude. https://www.additudemag.com/slideshows/adhd-quotes-for-a-bad-day/

ADDitude ADHD Therapies. (2021, July 8th). *The Science Behind 'Tapping:' An Alternative Therapy for Focus, Concentration & Mood*. ADDitude. https://www.additudemag.com/eft-adhd-tap-away-negative-emotions/

American Academy of Sleep Education. (August 2020). *Healthy sleep habits*. https://sleepeducation.org/healthy-sleep/healthy-sleep-habits/

American Psychiatric Association. (Reviewed 2022, June). *What is ADHD?* https://www.psychiatry.org/patients-families/adhd/what-is-adhd

Attention Deficit Disorder Association. (2022, October 24). *ADHD and sleep: Problems and solutions*. ADHD & Sleep: Problems and Solutions - ADDA - Attention Deficit Disorder Association

Becker, S. P. (2020). ADHD and sleep: Recent advances and future directions. *Current opinion in psychology, 34, 50-56*. https://www.sciencedirect.com/science/article/abs/pii/S2352225 0X19301630?via%3Dihub

Brott, N. R., & Reddivari, A. K. R. (2019). *Doxylamine*. StatPearls Publishing. https://www.ncbi.nlm.nih.gov/books/NBK551646/#:~:text=D oxylamine%20is%20a%20medication%20used,over%2Dthe %2Dcounter%20medication

Cain, S. W., McGlashan, E. M., et al. (2020). Evening home lighting adversely impacts the circadian system and sleep. *Scientific reports*, *10*(1), 19110. https://www.nature.com/articles/s41598-020-75622-4

Carefoot, H. (2023, May 9). *I tried progressive muscle relaxation, a simple exercise to help you 'flex' your way to sleep.* Well and Good. https://www.wellandgood.com/progressive-muscle-relaxation-sleep/

Cohut, M. (April 11, 2019). *This is how sleep loss alters emotional perception.* Medical News Today. https://www.medicalnewstoday.com/articles/324937

CDC. (n.d.). *Treatment of ADHD.* Centers for Disease Control and Prevention. https://www.cdc.gov/ncbddd/adhd/treatment.html

CDC. (Reviewed 2022). *Sleep and Sleep Disorders.* Center for Disease Control and Prevention. https://www.cdc.gov/sleep/about_sleep/chronic_disease.html

Cleveland Clinic. (Updated 2021a, April 27). *Sleeping Pills.* https://my.clevelandclinic.org/health/drugs/15308-sleeping-pills

Cleveland Clinic. (Updated 2021b, April 27). *Shift work sleep disorder (SWSD).* Shift Work Sleep Disorder (SWSD): Symptoms & Treatment (clevelandclinic.org)

Cleveland Clinic. (Reviewed 2021c, April 29). *Parasomnias and disruptive sleep disorders.* Parasomnias: Causes, Symptoms, Types & Management (clevelandclinic.org)

Cleveland Clinic. (Reviewed 2023a, February 2). *Attention Deficit Hyperactivity Disorder.* Attention-Deficit/Hyperactivity Disorder (ADHD) (clevelandclinic.org)

Cleveland Clinic. (Updated 2023b, March 1). *Benzodiazepines (Benzos).* https://my.clevelandclinic.org/health/treatments/24570-benzodiazepines-benzos

Cleveland Clinic. (Updated 2023c, June 19). *Sleep*.
    https://my.clevelandclinic.org/health/articles/12148-sleep-
    basics

College of Physicians and Surgeons of Nova Scotia. (Reviewed 2022,
    March 25). *Benzodiazepines and Z-drugs*.
    https://cpsns.ns.ca/resource/benzodiazepines-and-z-drugs/

Cooper, J. (n.d.). *Screens and your sleep: The impact of nighttime
    use*. Sutter Health.
    https://www.sutterhealth.org/health/sleep/screens-and-your-
    sleep-the-impact-of-nighttime-
    use#:~:text=How%20Much%20is%20Too%20Much,other
    %20type%20of%20relaxing%20activity

Dahl, D. (Updated 2023, August 5). *ADHD quotes about the
    neurodivergent way of paying attention*. Everyday Power.
    https://everydaypower.com/adhd-quotes/

de Bellefonds, C. (2021, May 28). *How acupuncture can optimize
    sleep patterns and free you from insomnia*. Healthline.
    https://www.healthline.com/health/acupuncture-for-sleep

Dimitriu, A. (2021, October 21). *ADHD is not just lack of focus:
    The effects can be dangerous*. Psychology Today.
    https://www.psychologytoday.com/intl/blog/psychiatry-and-
    sleep/202110/adhd-is-not-just-lack-focus-the-effects-can-be-
    dangerous

Deshong, A. (Updated 2022, December 13). *Cognitive behavioral
    therapy for insomnia CBT-I*. Sleep Doctor.
    https://sleepdoctor.com/insomnia/cognitive-behavioral-
    therapy-insomnia/

Dodson, W. (Updated 2023, August 25). *ADHD and sleep problems:
    This is why you're always tired*. ADDitude.
    https://www.additudemag.com/adhd-sleep-disturbances-
    symptoms/

Duffy, M. (Updated 2017, March 12). *For Kids with Autism, Shifting to Daylight Saving Time is Time of Angst*. The Gazette. https://www.thegazette.com/health-care-medicine/for-kids-with-autism-shifting-to-daylight-saving-time-is-time-of-angst/

Falcone, D.R. (2023, October 9). *Why you should incorporate tea into your nighttime routine*. Sleep.com https://www.sleep.com/sleep-health/tea-for-sleeping

Foley, L. (Updated 2023, October 5). *Periodic Limb Movements Disorder*. Sleep Foundation. https://www.sleepfoundation.org/periodic-limb-movement-disorder#:~:text=syndrome%20and%20narcolepsy.-,What%20Is%20PLMD%3F,their%20lower%20limbs%20during%20sleep

Garey, J. (Reviewed 2023, October 30). *How to help teenagers get more sleep*. Child Mind Institute. https://childmind.org/article/help-teenagers-get-sleep/

Goldstein, A. N., & Walker, M. P. (2014). The role of sleep in emotional brain function. *Annual review of clinical psychology*, 10, 679-708. https://doi.org/10.1146/annurev-clinpsy-032813-153716

Greeting Ideas. (n.d.). *35 Inspiring ADHD quotes and sayings: ADHD Awareness Month*. 35 Inspiring ADHD Quotes and Sayings: ADHD Awareness Month (greetingideas.com)

Harvard Health Publishing. (2017, July 14). *The health hazards of insufficient sleep*. https://www.health.harvard.edu/staying-healthy/the-health-hazards-of-insufficient-sleep

HealthMatch. (Updated 2022, September 6). *How To Use Pressure Points To Help You Fall Asleep*. Insomnia. https://healthmatch.io/insomnia/pressure-points-to-help-fall-asleep

Harley, J. (2020, December 29). *Self-hypnosis for sleep: What it is and how to do it*. Mindset Health. https://www.mindsethealth.com/matter/hypnosis-for-sleep

Higuera, V. (Reviewed 2022, September 29). *What is melatonin? Dosage, side effects, sleep usage, and overdose risks.* Everyday Health. What Is Melatonin? (everydayhealth.com)

Hours, C., Recasens, C., & Baleyte, J. M. (2022). ASD and ADHD Comorbidity: What Are We Talking About? *Frontiers in psychiatry*, *13*, 837424. https://doi.org/10.3389/fpsyt.2022.837424

Intrepid Mental Wellness, LLC. (n.d.). *12 Essential oils for a better night's sleep.* https://www.intrepidmentalhealth.com/blog/12-essential-oils-for-a-better-nights-sleep

Jeraci, A.R. (n.d.a). *Yoga nidra and the five koshas.* Yoga International. https://yogainternational.com/article/view/yoga-nidra-and-the-five-koshas/

Jeraci, A.R. (n.d.b). *What is yoga nidra and its benefits.* Yoga International. https://yogainternational.com/article/view/5-benefits-of-yoga-nidra/

Johns Hopkins Medicine. (n.d.b). *Aromatherapy: Do essential oils really work?* https://www.hopkinsmedicine.org/health/wellness-and-prevention/aromatherapy-do-essential-oils-really-work#:~:text=What%20Is%20a%3F,emotional%20center%20of%20the%20brain

Johns Hopkins Medicine. (n.d.a) *Narcolepsy.* Narcolepsy | Johns Hopkins Medicine

Joiner, W. J. (2018). The neurobiological basis of sleep and sleep disorders. *Physiology*, *33*(5), 317-327. https://doi.org/10.1152/physiol.00013.2018

Kim, S. (2022, January 15). *Sleep hypnosis—What it is, How it works and who can benefit.* Newsweek 90. https://www.newsweek.com/sleep-hypnosis-definition-how-it-works-benefits-risks-1666924

Leavitt, J. (2022, November 30). *The 8 best breathing techniques for sleep*. Healthline. https://www.healthline.com/health/breathing-exercises-for-sleep

Lindberg, S. (2019, November 22). *What to know about autogenic training*. Healthline. https://www.healthline.com/health/mental-health/autogenic-training

Marshall, L. (March 23, 2022). *Get morning light, sleep better at night*. WebMd. https://www.webmd.com/sleep-disorders/features/morning-light-better-sleep

Mayo Clinic Staff. (October 15, 2016). *Insomnia*. Mayo Clinic. https://www.mayoclinic.org/diseases-conditions/insomnia/symptoms-causes/syc-20355167#:~:text=Chronic%20insomnia%20is%20usually%20a,Stress.

Mayo Clinic Staff. (2022a, June 8). *Sleep aids: Understand options sold without a prescription*. Mayo Clinic. https://www.mayoclinic.org/healthy-lifestyle/adult-health/in-depth/sleep-aids/art-20047860

Mayo Clinic Staff. (2022b, September 16). *Prescription sleeping pills: What's right for you?* Mayo Clinic. https://www.mayoclinic.org/diseases-conditions/insomnia/in-depth/sleeping-pills/art-2004395

McDermott, N. (2023, September 20). *CBD For Sleep: How It Works, Benefits And Risks*. Forbes Health. https://www.forbes.com/health/cbd/cbd-for-sleep/#:~:text=While%20more%20research%20is%20needed,to%20sleep%2C%E2%80%9D%20says%20Dr

Mind. (2021, April). *Sleeping pills and minor tranquillisers*. https://www.mind.org.uk/information-support/drugs-and-treatments/sleeping-pills-and-minor-tranquillisers/side-effects-of-benzodiazepines/

Miller, C. (Updated January 26, 2023). *What are non-stimulant medications for ADHD?* Child Mind Institute. https://childmind.org/article/what-are-nonstimulant-medications-for-adhd/

Miller, L. (Updated 2023, August 7). *Benzodiazepine Addiction: Signs, Effects, and Treatment.* American Addiction Centers. https://americanaddictioncenters.org/benzodiazepine

Mount Sinai. (n.d.). *Biofeedback.* https://www.mountsinai.org/health-library/treatment/biofeedback

Myhre, J. & Sifris, D. (Updated 2023, August 31). *Glycine: benefits, side effects, and risks.* Verywell *Health.* https://www.verywellhealth.com/glycine-overview-4583816

National Institute on Drug Abuse. (January 2014). *Stimulant ADHD Medications: Methylphenidate and Amphetamines.* https://www.poison.org/-/media/files/webpoisoncontrol/references-and-for-more-info/articles/2011dec/drugfactsstimulantadhd1.pdf

Neff. (n.d.). *Autism, ADHD, and sleep: An expert guide on neurodivergent sleep.* Neurodivergent Insights. https://neurodivergentinsights.com/blog/autism-adhd-and-sleep

Next Step 4 ADHD. (2020, March 13). *Parenting a child with ADHD: 5 tips for peaceful bedtime routines.* https://nextstep4adhd.com/5-tips-for-bedtime-adhd/

NIH. (Updated 2023, July 19). *Brain basics: Understanding sleep.* National Institute of Neurological Disorders and Stroke. https://www.ninds.nih.gov/health-information/public-education/brain-basics/brain-basics-understanding-sleep

National Institute of Occupational Health and Safety. (Reviewed April 13, 2023). *Effects of light on circadian rhythms.* Centers for Disease Control and Prevention. https://www.cdc.gov/niosh/work-hour-training-for-nurses/longhours/mod2/19.html

Nemours Kids Health. (n.d.). *Sleep study (polysomnogram)*.
    https://kidshealth.org/en/parents/sleep-
    study.html#:~:text=A%20sleep%20study%20(also%20called
    ,functions%20while%20a%20child%20sleeps

NHS. (Reviewed 2023, February 28). *Acupuncture*.
    https://www.nhs.uk/conditions/acupuncture/

NYU Langone. (n.d.). Diagnosing sleep disorders in children.
    https://nyulangone.org/conditions/sleep-disorders-in-
    children/diagnosis

Pacheco, D., Dimitriu, A. (September 22, 2023). *ADHD and sleep*.
    Sleep Foundation. ADHD and Sleep Problems: How Are
    They Related? | Sleep Foundation

Pedersen, Traci. (2023, June 14). *Can you take melatonin if you have
    ADHD?* Healthline.
    https://www.healthline.com/health/adhd/melatonin-and-adhd

Peters, B. (2022, June 19). *How cognitive behavioral therapy for
    insomnia (CBT-I) works*. Very Well Health.
    https://www.verywellhealth.com/what-is-cognitive-
    behavioral-therapy-for-insomnia-cbti-3015310

Petre, A. (Updated 2023, March 29). *10 natural sleep aids for better
    sleep in 2023*. Healthline. 10 of the Best Natural Sleep Aids
    in 2022 (healthline.com)

Ramirez, A., Garner, C., Krutsch, K., & Hale, T. (n.d.). *ADHD medications and breastfeeding*. Infant Risk Center. https://www.infantrisk.com/content/adhd-medications-and-breastfeeding#:~:text=It%20is%20rare%20that%20a,breastfeeding%20to%20take%20a%20medication.&text=Multiple%20studies%20have%20demonstrated%20that,her%20ADHD%20medication%20as%20prescribed

Shen, C., Luo, Q., Chamberlain, S. R., et al. (2020). What is the link between attention-deficit/hyperactivity disorder and sleep disturbance? A multimodal examination of longitudinal relationships and brain structure using large-scale population-based cohorts. *Biological psychiatry*, 88(6), 459-469. https://www.sciencedirect.com/science/article/pii/S0006322320313810

Silver, L. (Updated July 13, 2022). *ADHD Neuroscience 101*. ADDitude. https://www.additudemag.com/adhd-neuroscience-101/#:~:text=ADHD%20was%20the%20first%20disorder,is%20synthesized%20within%20the%20brain

Sinfield, J. (Updated 2022, November 14). *The ADHD vs. non-ADHD brain*. Very Well Mind. https://www.verywellmind.com/the-adhd-brain-4129396

Sleep Cycle. (2021, November 30). *The benefits of meditation for sleep*. The benefits of meditation for sleep - Sleep Cycle

Sleep Health Foundation. (2023, September 4). *Cognitive behavioral therapy for insomnia (CBT-I)*. https://www.sleephealthfoundation.org.au/sleep-disorders/cognitive-behavioural-therapy-for-insomnia-cbt-i

Stanford Medicine. (n.d.). *Delayed sleep phase syndrome.* Stanford
    Medicine. Delayed Sleep Phase Syndrome | Stanford Health
    Care

Stein, M. (Updated August 10, 2023). *Sleep and ADHD medication
    use: A clinician's guide to mitigating side effects in children.*
    ADDitude. https://www.additudemag.com/sleep-and-adhd-
    medication-side-effects-
    children/#:~:text=One%20study3%20that%20analyzed,onse
    t%20of%20about%2012%20minutes

Suni, E. & Singh, A. (Updated 2023, October 12). *How much sleep
    do you need?* Sleep Foundation.
    https://www.sleepfoundation.org/how-sleep-works/how-
    much-sleep-do-we-really-need

Suni, E., & Rehman, A. (Updated 2023, October 5). *Natural Sleep
    Aids.* Sleep Foundation.
    https://www.sleepfoundation.org/sleep-aids/natural-sleep-aids

Tina, S. (2018, November 30). *JetBlue founder David Neeleman
    weighs in on the positives of ADHD.* Industry Buzz. JetBlue
    Founder David Neeleman Weighs in on the Positives of
    ADHD - IB (industry-buzz.com)

Tosini, G. (2022). Blue-light-blocking lenses in eyeglasses: a question
    of timing. *Optometry and vision science: official publication
    of the American Academy of Optometry,* 99(3), 228. doi:
    10.1097/OPX.0000000000001866

Tourville, J. (2023). *"Tap" your way to less stress and better sleep.* Women's Health Network. https://www.womenshealthnetwork.com/fatigue-and-insomnia/tapping-for-stress-relief-insomnia/#:~:text=Tapping%20is%20a%20self%20care,to%20give%20tapping%20a%20try%3F

UCLA Health. (n.d.) *Sleep disorders. Sleep problems in teens.* https://www.uclahealth.org/medical-services/sleep-disorders/patient-resources/patient-education/sleep-and-teens

Wirth, J. (Updated August 24, 2023). *ADHD statistics and facts in 2023.* Forbes. https://www.forbes.com/health/mind/adhd-statistics/

Wu, J. (n.d.). *Insomnia 101: How the brain regulates sleep and how you can help.* Dr. Jade Wu. https://drjadewu.com/blog/2018/9/25/insomnia-101-how-the-brain-regulates-sleep-and-how-you-can-help#:~:text=Similarly%2C%20if%20every%20night%20you,is%20called%20%E2%80%9Cconditioned%20arousal.%E2%80%9D